"Discipling, mentoring, and guiding our children toward a trusting, thriving, and loving relationship with God is a monumental, incredible, and essential task for Christian parents! Tim's passion for seeing God's Word passed on to future generations comes through as he provides parents with practical, hands-on, engaging, and easy-to-use family devotions. Who wouldn't like to have fire, food, money, dark rooms, flashlights, and light sticks while learning about what God is telling us in Scripture? This is a must-have for a parent's devotional library!"

Danny Huerta, MSW, LCSW, vice president of parenting and youth at Focus on the Family and family therapist

"Hey, Mom and Dad (or youth worker)! Get ready to zap, laugh, explore, explode, build, slime, slide, and think new thoughts with those kids you love so much. Tim Shoemaker has a unique gift for delivering biblical truths and critical life lessons in wacky, relevant, and unforgettable ways."

Jay Payleitner, national speaker and bestselling author of *52 Things Kids Need from a Dad* and *What If God Wrote Your Bucket List?*

"This book is fabulous! The devotions are memorable, unique, fun for all ages, engaging, and not complicated. They're well explained, so you won't be overwhelmed. Your kids won't be either—the devotions are long enough and deep enough to think about without needing to be a Bible scholar. As Tim explains in his important opening statement about how to lead devotions so you'll be consistent, that's not the point of short devotions. How refreshing! You can lead these successfully. Mostly, though, I love this book because Tim chose to emphasize very important and relevant truths for today's kids living in chaotic times. I'm impressed! I'd love to hear the discussions you have after you drop Jell-O brains, dig up buried ground beef, and try to melt Ivory soap in the microwave. You and your children are going to learn so much!"

Kathy Koch, PhD, founder and president of Celebrate Kids, Inc. and author of *8 Great Smarts* and *Start with the Heart*

"Two things undermine family devotions—kids being bored and parents not knowing how to do it. Tim Shoemaker knocks both of these problems out of the park with unique, attention-grabbing activities and clear, concise instructions. Start enjoying family devotions!"

Rob Currie, PhD, professor of psychology at Judson University and author of *Hungry for More of God*

D1569874

"I highly recommend *The Very Best, Hands-On, Kinda Dangerous Family Devotions* from Tim Shoemaker. This book captures the creativity and practical application of what Tim has taught to thousands of men at our Iron Sharpens Iron conferences over the last ten years. If you want to have a blast, literally, teaching your children or youth group biblical truth, there is no better resource."

Tom Cheshire, founder of Relevant Practical Ministry for Men (RPM)

"As a dad and a pastor, I am thankful for the wisdom and creativity of Tim Shoemaker's devotionals. I will not only use this book for my own family's devotions but also our youth group. No more rolling of the eyes from bored kids while doing devotions! I recommend this book to every parent, pastor, and youth leader. If you are looking to have attention-keeping and life-impacting devos, these are it. They are biblically rooted and FUN to do! Be dangerous!"

Pastor Jim Olsen, First Baptist Church, Pine Island

"Today, when all kinds of technology and digital opportunities compete for your kids' time and attention, even the most committed parents can find family devotions challenging. Good news: *The Very Best, Hands-On, Kinda Dangerous Family Devotions* is exactly what you need to make family devotions exciting, relevant, and life-changing. This how-to book deals with the spiritual issues kids face today with a totally over-the-top style that will have your kids asking you when you're having family devotions again. It will revolutionize your family devotions and help you make this tricky aspect of raising godly kids fun—and even a little dangerous at the same time."

Dr. Dale McElhinney, licensed psychologist and author

"I have watched Tim Shoemaker present these unique and fun object lessons at workshops for many years now. What I am most impressed with is that every guy who attends his presentation comes away with the feeling that 'I can do that!' In a time when family interaction has devolved into scrolling social media together, Tim offers a unique way to present biblical lessons in a fun and interactive way. A valuable tool for any father's family tool belt!"

Roy Abbott, president of Focal Point Ministries
and Iron Sharpens Iron Men's Conferences

THE VERY BEST, HANDS-ON, KINDA DANGEROUS FAMILY DEVOTIONS

52 ACTIVITIES YOUR KIDS WILL NEVER FORGET

TIM SHOEMAKER

Revell

a division of Baker Publishing Group
Grand Rapids, Michigan

© 2019 by Tim Shoemaker

Published by Revell
a division of Baker Publishing Group
PO Box 6287, Grand Rapids, MI 49516-6287
www.revellbooks.com

Printed in the United States of America

Library of Congress Cataloging-in-Publication Data
Names: Shoemaker, Tim, author.
Title: The very best, hands-on, kinda dangerous family devotions : 52 activities
    your kids will never forget / Tim Shoemaker.
Description: Grand Rapids : Baker Publishing Group, 2019.
Identifiers: LCCN 2018045152 | ISBN 9780800735555 (pbk.)
Subjects: LCSH: Christian education—Home training. | Christian education of
    children. | Object-teaching. | Families—Religious life.
Classification: LCC BV1590 .S56 2019 | DDC 249—dc23
LC record available at https://lccn.loc.gov/2018045152

19 20 21 22 23 24 25   7 6 5 4 3 2 1

To Andy and Laura, Mark and Sarah,
and Luke and Beth

May this book be one more tool to help you teach
the next generation about God,
and the principles he's given us to live by.

"Open my eyes that I may see wonderful things
in your law." (Ps. 119:18)

But as for you, be strong and do not give up,
for your work will be rewarded.

2 CHRONICLES 15:7

CONTENTS

———— OBJECT LESSONS AND ACTIVITIES ————

1. TP Blaster 29

THEME: Holy Spirit control / walking in the Spirit versus living in our own power

We'll convert a leaf blower to shoot toilet paper nearly thirty feet in the air. You'll be laughing so hard the first time you use it you may need a little of the TP yourself. This will launch a discussion about walking in our own power versus walking in the power of the Holy Spirit.

2. Electro-Pickle 34

THEME: Battle between old and new nature / defeating the old nature

When an ordinary dill pickle is connected to an electric current, it lights up and flickers like there's a battle going on inside. This makes a perfect opener to discuss the fight that goes on between our old and new nature—and how to end the battle for good.

ground beef on a bun. Nobody will argue which one is more appetizing. This gets a discussion cooking about the tough things we face in life. Sometimes God has to put us on the grill and turn up the heat to make us better, more appetizing as a person, so we can truly nourish others.

13. Catching Fire 90

THEME: Burning for God with passion versus being passive in our faith

Have the kids make an X on a piece of wood using toothpaste and two other pastes that come in tubes. Then put a lighter to each one—and they'll find only one of them will catch fire. This will ignite a discussion about the kind of person they want to be—one who is unaffected when they hear the Word or one who burns in dedication and obedience to God.

14. Surf's Up 95

THEME: Real friends—how to be one / what to look for in one

Imagine a piece of plywood balanced on top of four balloons. Now get one of the kids to balance on it. Definitely harder than it looks, but with the help of a friend or two, very doable. This starts things off on the right foot for a talk about genuine friends, how they help us stand strong and stay balanced in a society full of hot air.

15. Snow Fort 101

THEME: Doing things that count for eternity

For obvious reasons, this one only works outdoors, in the winter, and in places where you'd get enough snow to make a fort. Piles at the edge of a parking lot work well. Make a snow fort as big and elaborate as you can. Then grab some cocoa and talk to your kids about how everything they labored to build will melt away in a matter of weeks.

16. Christianity and the $2 Bill 105

THEME: A true relationship with Christ changes everything and should make us inseparable from Christ

$2 bills are rare, and a closer look should remind us of some important things about the Christian life.

4/21

A Quick Key for Parents

 Activities with this symbol are a little more on the dangerous side
and will require some extra caution on your part. Additional safety
tips and reminders are also included in these lessons.

 Activities with this symbol may not be age appropriate for younger
children. Please use your discretion when teaching these lessons.

INTRODUCTION

When my boys were growing up, I took them to a stock car race for a family devotional. Not a NASCAR race, just a regional event for weekend racers.

We did what most guys do at a stock car race. We each picked "our" car on the opening lap and cheered them on once they got the green flag. We totally enjoyed the races . . . the bumping, the action at the turns, and the dramatic finishes. We didn't talk at all about spiritual things—until the drive home.

"Tell me what you saw tonight," I said. "Boil it down. What was going on?"

I let them think for a moment.

"A bunch of men driving around in a circle," one of my sons said. "Trying to get ahead of each other."

"And most of the drivers ended up right where they started," another added. "With nothing."

I couldn't have asked for a better, more perfect entrance ramp to the things I wanted to talk to them about.

"And that's how most men live their entire lives," I said. "They're going around in circles, trying to get ahead of each other—but in the end they end up just where they started. With nothing."

I let that sink in for a moment. "You have a choice. You can go the way of the world . . . and if you do, get ready for a lifetime on the oval track. But I want to encourage you to take the journey of life with God. He's got a plan for you. A person for you to become. He won't just lead you in circles."

The same is true for your kids. As parents, we protect our kids, we provide for them, and we prepare them for the future. Teaching our kids spiritually is essential for all three of those things.

I want to help you get on track teaching your kids about God—and the principles he's given us to live by. More than just get you on the road with this, I want to help you shift spiritual training for the kids into high gear. You can do this. As a mom or dad. As a couple. As a single parent. As a grandparent. You can effectively teach your kids spiritual truth. You'll find it's easy. Powerful. And best of all . . . unforgettable.

So buckle up, my friend. Let's shift into high gear.

ENDING THE STOP AND START SYNDROME

I live in the Chicago area, and every winter our roads get potholes. Hit one of those and you can lose control, knock the alignment out on your car, get a flat, or damage a rim.

Maybe you've hit a few potholes in your attempts to lead family devotions before. You started with good intentions, but somewhere along the line you end up on the side of the road—going nowhere.

I've hit my fair share of potholes and was "stop and start" with family devotions until I discovered how well the kids responded to object lessons and activities like you'll find in this book. Ideally, once you start family devotions, you'll want to be consistent. Let me race through fourteen tips to help you avoid some of the common potholes that can slow you down, make you suddenly swerve off course, or bring your family devotions to a stop.

1. Remember, these are devotionals—not Bible studies.

This book is packed with object lessons and activities—each designed to get a nugget of truth across to your kids. The whole idea is to do something with the family—relatively quickly—and in a way that both you and the kids enjoy. Resist the urge to draw these out into long "sit down and listen" lessons. The kids won't enjoy them, and neither will you. If that happens, the likelihood that you'll quit goes way up.

2. Follow up the activity with a brief tie-in to a biblical principle.

Generally, that tie-in can be done in five minutes. Go longer if the kids ask questions, but avoid the trap of getting repetitive. If you give a speech, you'll lose them. The point is to stop before they get bored and you'll be much more likely to do family devotions next week.

3. Have family devotions once a week, but make them good.

I know, once a week doesn't sound like much. But that's fifty-two nuggets of truth etched in their hearts and minds every year. If you try to do active, object lesson–oriented family devotions daily, you'll likely run out of ideas or skimp on the prep, and the kids won't get as much out of it. Either way, the tendency to burn out and quit is high.

If you're already in the habit of leading the kids in some kind of devotional daily—great. Just add something active and visual, like what you'll find in this book, once a week.

4. Pick a time that works best for their schedules.

If the kids are missing something important to them, it will be hard to hold their attention no matter what you do. If you don't hold their attention, you'll probably quit.

5. If the kids ask a question that stumps you, don't let it stop your lesson.

Whatever you do, don't just guess at an answer. Tell them you'll have to get back to them. Then search the Scriptures, talk to your pastor, or whatever. As long as you get back to them, you're fine. And remember, there are some questions only God can answer.

6. If the kids seem bored, don't give up.

They may be rebelling on the whole thing a bit. Hang in there. Pick short, fun devotionals. They'll come around.

7. If the kids have a hard time settling down, go with the flow.

Avoid ordering them to be quiet. There are worse things than your kids thinking that learning about God can be a fun time.

8. When tying in the lesson, incorporate food whenever possible.

If they're snacking, they'll be more patient. Less distracted. Their hands are busy, and so are their mouths. They'll enjoy the lesson—and so will you. When everyone is enjoying the time, you'll be more likely to keep going with weekly family devotions.

9. Keep this book in front of you when you tie in the lesson.

If you try to do a devotional lesson without the book, you'll likely go long and still miss key points. Your kids' focus will drift, and *wham*—you just hit a pothole. Also, if you try to remember everything, you'll have to put in so much prep time that your chances of quitting go way up. Kids don't mind if you use a book. But here's the key: jot notes in the margins. Highlight sections. The kids need to know you've studied. Prepared.

If they think you're looking at the chapter for the first time as you go over it with them, they'll think the lesson you're teaching isn't all that important to you—or that you think they're not smart enough to notice you didn't prepare. Either way, you've just hit another pothole.

10. Go with the kids you have.

If your kids have friends over, you can still have family devotions as long as you don't embarrass your kids. Keep the devotional activity part fun and your talk time short. Most kids are really open to—even hungry for—some adult interaction in their lives.

And if one of your kids is out of the house for some event, do the devotions with the kids you have. Some weeks you'll never have devotions if you wait until everybody is together. Just catch up later with the one who missed the devotions.

11. Beware of crazy schedules.

Sometimes the potholes are all the activities and sports we sign our kids up for. There's hardly any time left to teach them God's truth. You may want to rethink how many extracurricular activities you allow for the kids.

12. Reinforce the application throughout the week after devotions.

Be smart about it. Don't use this like a club on the kids, such as: "Katy—talk nice to your sister! That's exactly what we were talking about in our family devotions yesterday." Too much of that and kids will think family devotions are just part of your agenda to modify their behavior. A better practice is to call it on yourself. "Hey, kids, did you hear how I just talked to Mom? That was wrong, and it was exactly what I was talking about yesterday." Then tell your wife you're sorry. The kids will learn by your example.

13. If you have multiple ages present, target the oldest.

This is critical. If you try to make sure you teach in such a way that your youngest understands everything, your oldest will think family devotions are "kid stuff." You'll have a really difficult time pulling the older ones in after that. Also, your older kids are closer to the danger, and you have less time to get through to them before they leave the house. For all these reasons, target your older kids with the content of your devotions and how you present it. You can always give a little extra explanation to your younger ones later—or, better yet, let your older kids help explain.

14. Be careful to put the Word into practice yourself.

If you tell your kids how important it is to follow God's principles for living, be sure you're striving to live that out in your own life—especially at home. If you get sloppy—especially with how you treat your mate, if you're married—you'll lose your kids' respect. If they don't respect you, they won't receive what you tell them in family devotions time. You'll sense that, and it will make it *really* hard to keep going with family devotions.

No matter how much you try to avoid the "stop and start" syndrome, likely you'll run into weeks when life gets in the way and you skip family devotions. Don't beat yourself up. Get back at it the following week.

Remember, leading family devotions is one of the greatest ways we can *prepare*, *provide*, and *protect* our kids in this stage of their lives—and for their future. Don't let a pothole stop you.

OBJECT LESSONS
and ACTIVITIES

TP Blaster

THEME: Holy Spirit control / walking in the Spirit versus living in our own power

THINGS YOU'LL NEED

- ☐ Leaf blower—the more powerful the better, with an oval-shaped snout opening
- ☐ Extension cord (25 feet is ideal) and access to electrical outlet if leaf blower is electric
- ☐ 4-inch paint roller; pick the smoothest moving one you can find
- ☐ Duct tape—or for a very sturdy mounting, a drill, a bit, and two bolts with nuts to attach the paint roller handle to the end of the leaf blower snout
- ☐ Flat metal file if the paint roller handle is rounded
- ☐ At least six single-ply, thousand-sheet rolls of toilet paper

Advance Prep

If you already have a leaf blower, great. If you're purchasing one, make sure that the end of the snout where the air blows out is oval, not round, so you'll get a more concentrated blast of air directed at the TP.

Buy a really free-wheeling roller. The cheap ones don't spin as easily or quickly, and you don't want anything inhibiting your demonstration. I went to a paint shop to find one. If the handle is rounded, it will be tougher to mount to the snout without it tipping from side to side. Take a metal file and flatten out a spot on the handle. That will keep the roller mounted square—which means the roll of TP will be held in the perfect position.

Now position the roller at the end of the leaf blower snout, and either wrap with duct tape to fasten or drill through both the handle and the snout. Slide the bolts through, snug down the nuts, and you're ready to roll—or better yet, unroll!

Make sure the tube in the TP roll is nice and round for a free-flowing experience. It's a good idea to make sure each of the rolls has been unrolled a few turns before you start. Generally, the manufacturer glues down the leading edge.

Place the tube on the roller. It won't fit snugly—you'll need to hold the blower on a bit of an angle so the TP doesn't fall off. The end of the paper should roll off the tube away from the leaf blower.

Okay—give it a try. Your kids are going to love this as much as you do!

Running the Activity

The TP Blaster should be plugged in and ready to go, but drape a towel over it to keep it hidden for now. Now call the kids over.

Hand a roll of toilet paper to one of the kids, explaining that they'll be in a race to unroll the paper. They can use their two forefingers as an axle to twirl the paper off the tube, or they can use one finger as an axle and use the other hand to pull the paper off the tube. If they choose the second method, explain that if they rip the paper three times they'll be disqualified. Demo this for them so they know exactly how to do it.

If you have enough kids, mention that one of them will work together with you, but you'll have to unload two rolls instead of just one—and you'll use a different method to do that.

Now give the kid unrolling the TP by hand a head start. Once they begin, uncover the leaf blower and hand it to the kid helping you. Load a roll of TP on the paint roller, and show him or her how to hold the leaf blower at an angle so the TP roll doesn't slide off. Now you're set . . . turn on the leaf blower.

Get the next roll ready and pop it on as soon as the first one is done.

Teaching the Lesson

The one unrolling the TP by hand was working as hard as they could, trying not to become disqualified. This is how many people try to live the Christian life. Sometimes we're working so hard, just trying not to mess up.

- To be the kind of Christian we should be
- To be the kind of son or daughter we should be
- To be a good brother or friend or student or whatever

The truth is we don't feel we can do much more than we are doing now. And sometimes even when we try our best, we still mess up—or think we could have done better.

But that's where we need something beyond ourselves . . . the power of the Holy Spirit to help us. The modified leaf blower represents the work of the Holy Spirit in our lives. You didn't expect that we'd have something like this leaf blower to unroll the TP—and probably didn't have any idea it would be so effective. And that's how it is with the Holy Spirit. When we give the Holy Spirit control in our lives, he does the unexpected. The unforeseeable. Often, he changes our hearts.

If we really desire to give the Holy Spirit control so he can change us and help us be the person we should be through all circumstances, we need to let him lead.

Since we are living by the Spirit, let us follow the Spirit's leading in every part of our lives. (Gal. 5:25 NLT)

Letting the Spirit lead is often as simple as *asking* him to lead . . . and then following when he does.

Why don't we follow the Spirit's leading in every part of our lives? Sometimes it boils down to us wanting to do whatever it is we want to do.

- If we're in a bad mood, sometimes we don't want to change.
- If we're mad at someone, we don't really want to forgive them.
- If we're lusting after someone, we don't want to turn off the fantasy.
- If we're doing something wrong, sometimes we don't want to stop.

All of these examples are old nature things—the very things the Holy Spirit wants to help us overcome. If we want to experience the power of the Holy Spirit working in our lives, often it means we need to exercise some self-control as well. Sometimes that means controlling ourselves enough to ask God for help.

> A person without self-control
> is like a city with broken-down walls. (Prov. 25:28 NLT)

Think about ancient times and a city with broken-down walls. How safe was someone who lived in a city like that?

People living in a city without walls were vulnerable to attack. To raiders that would come in to steal and destroy. How are you vulnerable to danger when you don't practice self-control? Can you think of an example?

Sometimes self-control itself is hard. Sometimes we feel we have so little self-control. God can help us with that as well. One of the fruit of the Spirit, one of the things the Holy Spirit produces in our lives, is *self-control*.

> But the Holy Spirit produces this kind of fruit in our lives: love, joy, peace, patience, kindness, goodness, faithfulness, gentleness, and self-control. (Gal. 5:22–23 NLT)

Living the Christian life to the fullest isn't something God intends for us to do on our own, solely with our own power. He has given us the Holy Spirit.

Summing It Up

We need to give the Holy Spirit permission to work in our lives. To change our hearts. Our desires. To give us more self-control. And we need to exercise self-control ourselves. This is a real key to helping us live more like a Christian and keeping us out of danger. Without it, we're vulnerable to attacks from the enemy.

> So be careful how you live. Don't live like fools, but like those who are wise. Make the most of every opportunity in these evil days. Don't act thoughtlessly, but understand what the Lord wants you to do. Don't be drunk with wine, because that will ruin your life. Instead, be filled with the Holy Spirit. (Eph. 5:15–18 NLT)

> So I say, let the Holy Spirit guide your lives. Then you won't be doing what your sinful nature craves. (Gal. 5:16 NLT)

God isn't looking to rob us of fun. God gives us the Holy Spirit to *rescue* us from things that are wrong, from things that can hurt us, from things that come from our enemy, the devil and his demons.

God gives us his Holy Spirit to make changes inside us, in our hearts. He uses the Holy Spirit to do things in and through us that we could never predict. Things that would be impossible on our own.

So when we're struggling with our attitude, or with sin in any way, let's remember to exercise a little self-control . . . and let's remember to give the Holy Spirit permission to make changes in us. As we do that, we'll find that our walk as a Christian will get stronger.

- We won't mess up as much.
- We'll have fewer regrets.

And each time we give the Holy Spirit control, we'll be growing more and more into the person God wants us to be, so we can accomplish the good plans he has for us.

Electro-Pickle

THEME: Battle between old and new nature / defeating the old nature

⚠️ THINGS YOU'LL NEED

- ☐ Lamp cord with plug. If you are going to the hardware store, a simple, light-duty extension cord works fine. Just get a short cord that looks just like a lamp cord. Six feet is more than long enough.
- ☐ Two steel nails, about 2 or 2½ inches long with normal heads (not finishing nails)
- ☐ Pliers or wire cutters to cut and strip lamp cord
- ☐ Utility knife
- ☐ Electrical tape
- ☐ Jar of large dill pickles (ideally 3 to 4 inches long)
- ☐ Paper plate
- ☐ Access to an electrical outlet
- ☐ Power strip or another extension cord (optional)

Advance Prep

Clip the socket (the female end, which is opposite of the end that goes into the wall) off the extension or lamp cord with the pliers or wire cutters. Separate the two wires (one is positive, one is negative) in the cord for a length of six or eight inches. Do this by making a small cut in the plastic housing between the wires and pulling them apart.

Next, strip about one inch of the plastic housing from each of these ends to expose the strands of wire inside. Twist each bundle of wires between your thumb and forefinger like you are winding a toy so the wires form a single strand.

Wrap one twisted wire strand around each nail just below the head, then cover the wire and the nail head completely with electrical tape. The other one to two inches of the nail, including the tip, should be exposed. If you're comfortable soldering, you can solder the wire onto the nail before covering it with electrical tape.

As with every object lesson, you'll want to test this before trying it with the kids.

KEEP IT SAFE

Here are six quick safety precautions that I really hope I don't need to point out—but probably should just in case.

1. Be sure the nails are properly inserted into a pickle *before* plugging the cord into an outlet.
2. Don't let the exposed nails contact each other—or any person—while the cord is plugged in.
3. Don't do this experiment anywhere around water—like near a sink.
4. Don't touch the pickle while you are electrocuting it.
5. Never leave the pickle unattended while you're electrocuting it.
6. After you're done, don't leave the unplugged cord and nail contraption around for your kids to mess with. Toss the pickle out and pocket the cord.

Electrocuting the Pickle

- Select a pickle from the jar, blot off some of the juice, and set it on a paper plate.
- Insert one nail into each end of the pickle so the nail tips are aiming toward each other but are NOT touching. The nails should be inserted up to the electrical tape if possible.
- Plug in the lamp cord. If you are using a power strip, plug into the power strip and flip the switch to the "on" position.
- Within seconds you'll likely hear sizzling noises coming from the pickle, and you may start to see some smoke or steam escape from one of the ends. Then you should see a flash of light inside the pickle. Suddenly, you'll have what looks like a fireworks grand finale going on inside the pickle. This will look even better in a darkened room.
- Okay, unplug the pickle—you're ready to teach the lesson!

Now, one other safety note. If you or your spouse has reservations about this one because "it's dangerous," I totally get that. But the key is training. You leave your car keys on the kitchen table and don't worry about the kids taking your car for a joyride, right? It's a matter of training.

This is an important lesson, and rather than miss the truth of it because of the danger of this, do a little extra training with the kids. Explain that you'll electrocute a pickle whenever they want. If they want to show friends, they can just ask you, and you'll do the demo. And if you make them that promise . . . be sure you live up to it. Avoid stalling if they want to see it again.

Remind them that today's demo is dangerous and that you don't want them trying it on their own. You want them to understand that you're trusting them enough to do some pretty cool demos with them, but if they start abusing that, you'll have to go back to Bible picture books.

Running the Activity

Get the kids together and tell them they're going to witness the electrocution of a pickle. Pull out the pickle jar and let them select their victim.

After making sure the cord is unplugged from the power source, insert the nails, being sure the nail tips aren't touching each other. Also be sure to go over the safety rules with the kids. After the pickle is sitting on the plate and you're sure nobody is touching it, plug it in. Dim the lights to add to the effect. You won't want the room completely dark, though, or you may not be able to see the cord to unplug it.

Unplug the cord from the outlet after the pickle has been lit up for no more than ten seconds. The pickle will get hot and may start to burn if you leave it plugged in too long.

Teaching the Lesson

It looked like a battle was taking place inside the pickle. Imagine you were somehow transported inside the skin of that pickle while that was going on. That would be a really nasty place to be.

What we saw going on inside the pickle is sort of like a battle that often goes on inside a Christian. Anybody know what I'm talking about?

There is a *negative* influence in all of us, what the Bible calls our "old nature," that wants to live exactly opposite of how a Christian should live. But we also have a *positive* influence—the Holy Spirit—working in us to create a "new nature," to make us more and more like Christ. The light show inside the pickle looked pretty cool, but there is nothing fun about the spiritual battle that goes on inside us.

> The sinful nature wants to do evil, which is just the opposite of what the Spirit wants. And the Spirit gives us desires that are the opposite of what the sinful nature desires. These two forces are constantly fighting each other, so you are not free to carry out your good intentions. (Gal. 5:17 NLT)

The Bible describes part of what our old nature is all about.

> When you follow the desires of your sinful nature, the results are very clear: sexual immorality, impurity, lustful pleasures, idolatry, sorcery, hostility, quarreling, jealousy, outbursts of anger, selfish ambition, dissension, division, envy, drunkenness, wild parties, and other sins like these. Let me tell you again, as I have before, that anyone living that sort of life will not inherit the Kingdom of God. (vv. 19–21 NLT)

- Anybody recognize these battles? Selfishness, anger, arguing, jealousy, lust?
- In a battlefield situation, there are generally casualties. Soldiers get hurt, crippled, or worse. How can losing a battle with the old nature hurt us or change our lives in bad ways?

War is brutal. The enemy wants to kill, destroy, or imprison the opposition. That's what the devil wants to do to us.

God isn't looking to rob us of fun. God gives us the Holy Spirit to rescue us from things that are wrong, from things that can hurt us. He wants to protect us from things that come from our enemy, the devil and his demons. Some of these things can be fun for a time, but they come with a high cost.

Look at the things God wants to give us through the Holy Spirit.

But the Holy Spirit produces this kind of fruit in our lives: love, joy, peace, patience, kindness, goodness, faithfulness, gentleness, and self-control. There is no law against these things! (vv. 22–23 NLT)

The Holy Spirit wants to change our lives for the better, but if we stay in this area of conflict, we're in a really miserable place. We're consumed and frustrated by things we really want to do but know we shouldn't. Maybe we're racked with guilt about things we've done or are doing, or attitudes we have that we know we shouldn't.

Summing It Up

Somebody once described the battle inside a Christian as two dogs fighting. The dog we feed is the one that wins.

There is an uncomfortable battle between our old nature and the new work God wants to do in us through his Holy Spirit. But we don't have to stay there.

Ask God to change your heart. As we give him permission to change our hearts, he changes our desires and gives us new ones. Remember what we read in Galatians 5:17: "And the Spirit gives us desires that are the opposite of what the sinful nature desires" (NLT).

Next, let me encourage you to exercise self-control. Sometimes we have to have the strength to say no. That can be really hard, especially if you have the opportunity to do something that you'd really like to do—even though it is wrong. We need to keep feeding the part of us that wants to do the right thing. Remember, if you give in to your old nature, it will end up destroying you just like we did the pickle. It may not happen as quickly, but it will happen.

> Don't be misled—you cannot mock the justice of God. You will always harvest what you plant. Those who live only to satisfy their own sinful nature will harvest decay and death from that sinful nature. But those who live to please the Spirit will harvest everlasting life from the Spirit. So let's not get tired of doing what is good. At just the right time we will reap a harvest of blessing if we don't give up. (6:7–9 NLT)

Is there an area of your life that you need to talk to God about right now? Would you ask him to change your heart? And are you willing to do your part to exercise self-control?

Frankenstein Factor

THEME: **Dangers of messing with the sin we're to avoid**

THINGS YOU'LL NEED

☐ Official movie trailer for the 1931 black-and-white movie *Frankenstein* starring Boris Karloff. This is easily available on YouTube.

☐ If you want to make more of an event of watching the trailer, pick up the movie from an online source or from your local public library. If you choose this option, don't forget the pizza, popcorn, and so forth.

Advance Prep

If you've never watched any of the old Frankenstein "horror" movies from the 1930s and '40s . . . understand they're not very scary by today's standards. And all you'll really need to view with the kids is the official movie trailer for the 1931 *Frankenstein* film starring Boris Karloff, not the entire movie. Many DVD versions have the original theatrical trailer as a bonus feature—and of course, the trailer is an easy find on YouTube. It is melodramatic and hokey, which makes watching it fun.

Watch the trailer in advance to be sure you're okay with your kids seeing it. You can always wait until they're older. The trailer highlights the destruction and horror the monster creates, and you'll be able to start your discussion from there.

If you can get the DVD and would like to show clips from the film, I'd suggest these two scenes:

Scene 2, grave robbing. Show the portion of the scene where Dr. Frankenstein and his assistant dig up a grave to steal the body.

Scene 6, bringing the monster to life. Show just the part where Dr. Frankenstein uses lightning during the storm to bring the monster to life. End with the misguided doctor saying his legendary line, "It's moving. It's alive. It's alive . . . it's alive!"

Running the Activity

You can show the trailer on your smartphone, but when you go bigger, the whole thing seems to have a better effect. If you're showing it on your TV, get the room as dark as you can. Set up some candles to add to the creepy factor. Doing the entire devotional in this darkened setting—even your discussion time—will really set the mood.

Explain to the kids that they'll be looking at the original trailer for *Frankenstein* to discover a scary truth about the Christian life. Start with a basic overview of the Hollywood version of *Frankenstein*—and then continue on with the teaching portion of the lesson.

Nearly a century ago, this great-granddaddy of horror films raised goose bumps on the arms of terrified moviegoers across the United States. In *Frankenstein*, Dr. Frankenstein became obsessed with life and death. Specifically, the idea of creating life. The doctor employed a helper of questionable character, and together they dug up bodies as soon as the mourners left. Using body parts from a variety of corpses, Dr. Frankenstein stitched together his creation.

Using the power of an electrical storm and a bunch of whiz-bang gadgetry, he brought the "monster" to life. The monster eventually turned on his master and everyone else, wreaking havoc and disaster. Dr. Frankenstein couldn't control the monster—it had a life of its own.

We'll look at the original theatrical trailer (or some selected clips). Remember, this film is old. The sets are obvious, the script is predictable, the special effects are primitive, and the acting is the worst of all.

There is no terror factor to it anymore—at least not in the movie itself. The really *scary* thing is its parallel to the Christian life, and we'll talk about that after we've seen the trailer.

Are you ready? Let's view that trailer now.

Teaching the Lesson

Dr. Frankenstein was brilliant and talented, yet things went tragically wrong for him. He was obsessed with creating life—and he stole bodies to do it. He went against the advice of colleagues and the morals he'd been raised with.

- How "in control" did he feel when his creation came to life?
- What happened to his ability to control the monster?
- Who became the real master of the situation—Dr. Frankenstein or the monster?
- When the monster was unleashed, how destructive was it?

Let's read some selected verses from Romans 6 (NLT). Take special note to what it says about sin—and how we can become sin's slave.

Verse 6: "We know that our old sinful selves were crucified with Christ so that sin might lose its power in our lives. We are no longer slaves to sin."

Verse 7: "For when we died with Christ we were set free from the power of sin."

Verse 10: "When he died, he died once to break the power of sin. But now that he lives, he lives for the glory of God."

Verse 11: "So you also should consider yourselves to be dead to the power of sin and alive to God through Christ Jesus."

Verse 12: "Do not let sin control the way you live; do not give in to sinful desires."

Verse 13: "Do not let any part of your body become an instrument of evil to serve sin. Instead, give yourselves completely to God, for you were dead, but now you have new life. So use your whole body as an instrument to do what is right for the glory of God."

Verse 14: "Sin is no longer your master."

Verse 16: "Don't you realize that you become the slave of whatever you choose to obey? You can be a slave to sin, which leads to death, or you can choose to obey God, which leads to righteous living."

- There was a time when sin was our *master* and we were its *slave*. What does that suggest as far as who was really in control, us or our sin?
- What changed the situation? What event released us from sin's grip on our lives?
- Becoming a Christian released us from slavery to sin. Sin's power over us is declared dead by Jesus. Is it possible to revert back to sin being our master in some area of life? What does the passage say (Rom. 6:13–16)?
- If sin is our *master*, can we stop sinning any time we want to—like many kids tell themselves they can—without God's help?
- How might a person become hopelessly entangled in sin again?

Dr. Frankenstein just couldn't leave dead things alone. He should have left them buried and in the grave where they belonged. But he was obsessed with them. He dug them up and gave them life again. He gave them *power*.

- How is this like something we often do as Christians?
- When we get tangled up in wrong things again by thinking about them, looking at them, going back to old ways, and so on, which nature are we feeding—our old sin nature or our new nature?

The nature we feed is the one that will get stronger. There's an old saying that goes something like this: "If you let the devil ride, pretty soon he'll want to drive." There's another that says, "If you give the devil a toehold, he'll get a foothold and eventually a stronghold."

What do you think those sayings mean?

- Sin can become our master again. It can control us. Our thoughts. Our actions. Where is the danger in that?
- Like a monster, sin will destroy us. Rip us apart. Change us into something ugly. How quickly should we try to get away from sin's mastery over us?

Sometimes sin's grip on us is so strong we feel helpless. We live as though we are sin's slaves—powerless to break free. It's in those times that we have to rely even more on God. Only he can free us. We must ask him to give us new desires in our hearts.

> In my distress I prayed to the LORD,
>   and the LORD answered me and set me free. (Ps. 118:5 NLT)

Change doesn't always happen instantly. It often requires exercising self-discipline, setting up boundaries, and being honest with your parents as we help you work through it. You may fail many times, but you must get up quickly and keep fighting.

As God sets you free, you must remember his truth.

> But now you are free from the power of sin and have become slaves of God. Now you do those things that lead to holiness and result in eternal life. (Rom. 6:22 NLT)

In other words, when God frees you, stay away from the graveyard. Right?

Summing It Up

Dr. Frankenstein couldn't control his fascination with things declared dead—and he created a monster that he couldn't control. Of course, he *thought* he had things perfectly in control, at least at first. He created a monster that caused terror and heartache and loss.

- What about us? What type of wrong things are we allowing in our lives that may well be used to enslave us?
- How does that affect others, or how might it in the future if we don't change?

That's a scary thought. A whole lot scarier than the *Frankenstein* movie was. We need to ask God for help before it's too late, and keep on asking until we're released. And we need to stop playing in the graveyard. We're dead to sin, and dead things are best left buried. Right?

If God killed it, whether it was a wrong relationship, habit, attitude, addiction, whatever—we need to be careful not to go back there. Longing for something that is wrong is like powering the electrodes on Frankenstein's monster. Soon we'll bring it back to life—we will create a monster that can destroy us and hurt others!

Totaled

THEME: God forgives, but that doesn't mean there aren't consequences

THINGS YOU'LL NEED

- ☐ Safety glasses for everybody present, including you. You can pick these up cheap at the hardware store. And it's a good investment; you'll definitely use them for other object lessons in this book.
- ☐ Hammer (one will do, or you may opt for one hammer for each of the kids)
- ☐ Sledgehammer (optional, if pounding large items)
- ☐ Broom and other tools for cleanup
- ☐ Something to destroy . . . we'll talk about that in the next section

KEEP IT SAFE

Before anyone takes a swing with a hammer . . .

- Everybody present needs to be wearing safety glasses, even if they're only watching.
- If the item is small, have the kids take turns with the hammer. If you have more than one swinging a hammer at a time, you may end up with a nasty injury.
- If the item is really large, and you feel it is safe to have more than one using a hammer on it at a time, give each person a clear area or zone of the object to hit. Make sure each of the kids is spaced a safe distance from the others.

Advance Prep

The whole idea is that you and the kids are going to have fun totally destroying something with hammers. You'll need to figure out what that something is.

Drive around on garbage day and you'll likely find something at the curb that will work perfectly. Or ask friends or coworkers if they have an appliance or piece of furniture they'd like to donate for a little character-building lesson you want to teach your kids. People are generally happy to unload some of their clutter.

Try to get something that your kids would enjoy destroying. The bigger the better: TV, computer, microwave, refrigerator, or piece of furniture. You may even find someone who has a junker car parked in the driveway that they'd like to get rid of. The kids would never forget the day you demolished it as a family. Afterward you can have a wrecking company haul the car away—and usually you'll get a couple hundred bucks for scrap.

Running the Activity

Explain that you're going to destroy this thing in front of you and that they're going to help. Carefully go over the safety rules.

You'll need to set a time limit for the demolition activity. You're better off stopping the activity before they tire of it so you can talk with them. You can always let them take more swings at it after you tie in the spiritual truth.

When you're ready to talk to the kids about it, be sure to collect all the hammers first so they aren't still trying to pound on things.

Teaching the Lesson

Normally, it would be totally wrong for us to pound on something like this, would you agree? But we pounded on this today because I want to help you understand a very important principle from God's Word.

The Bible makes it clear that God forgives us for the wrong things we do if we confess those sins to him.

> But if we confess our sins to him, he is faithful and just to forgive us our sins and to cleanse us from all wickedness. (1 John 1:9)

That's really great news. But sometimes people misunderstand forgiveness. They think as long as God will forgive them, they can go ahead and do what they want—even though they know it is wrong. They figure that they'll just ask God to forgive them afterward. They think that's all there is to it, but they're forgetting something important.

Even though God forgives, there are still consequences.

There is often damage done that can't be fixed. Like when we pounded this (fill in the blank), we destroyed something. Nobody here is in trouble, but we've caused damage that can't simply be fixed. Even though we can be forgiven, it doesn't mean life can go on just as though we'd never sinned. Can anybody give me an example of how this is true?

- If someone says something unkind to another person, that person may still have very real hurt about what was said for years afterward—even though they've forgiven the person who said the hurtful things.

- If someone steals a car, the owner may forgive them but the state will still have to punish them. There are penalties and consequences for things we do that are wrong.

- If someone murders another person, there will be a trial and sentencing. Likely the murderer will go to jail, even if they said they were sorry and the victim's family forgave them.

- If someone lies to their mom or dad, their parent may forgive them, but there are still consequences. They may still be punished for the lie. And even if they aren't punished, there is still a penalty to be paid . . . and that is a loss of trust. Those parents will not be able to trust their son or daughter like they did before the lie.

- If someone sneaks and uses drugs or alcohol, their parents may forgive them, but the lasting effects of the drugs—or an addiction—may still haunt them.

Forgiveness removes the penalty for sin, but not necessarily the consequences.

Can you think of any Bible characters who messed up and were forgiven but still had to deal with the consequences of their sin?

- **Adam and Eve.** God forgave, but the consequences were unfathomable.
- **Moses killing the Egyptian.** God forgave, but there were consequences . . . like having to leave his home and live as a fugitive in the desert for forty years.
- **Moses striking the rock to get water from it.** God forgave, but Moses also lost his privilege to go into the Promised Land with his people.
- **Samson.** He sinned over and over again. God clearly forgave, but there were consequences. Samson lost his sight, his freedom, and finally his life because of the bad decisions he'd made.
- **David and Bathsheba.** God forgave, but there were massive consequences—including the death of their illegitimate baby.

Do you see how foolish it is to think, *I can do what I want—and just ask God to forgive me later?*

God forgives, but often the scars of our sin are tough to live with.

Summing It Up

Doing wrong things can be fun—just like when we pounded this (fill in the blank) with our hammers. We can be forgiven when we do wrong things, but we must be very careful not to be casual about sinning just because we know God will forgive us. There are consequences for sin. There are scars. Regrets. Things that are hard to live with. Our sin, even though forgiven, can cripple us emotionally.

Let me read you a verse from Proverbs, the book of wisdom.

> The highway of the upright avoids evil;
> those who guard their ways preserve their lives. (16:17)

Stay on track, kids. Stay on the right paths. Do the right things. By being careful about what you do and don't do, you're actually guarding your own life. You're protecting yourself from nasty consequences that come from choosing to do the wrong things.

The Right Combination

THEME: **There is absolute truth**

THINGS YOU'LL NEED

- ☐ At least one combination lock. If you have one lock for each of the kids, that would be even better.
- ☐ One pair of dice

Advance Prep

If you want to mess with the kids a little, memorize the combination for one of the locks—but don't let them know you've done so. Be sure you can identify that lock easily when you do this lesson with the kids.

Running the Activity

Hand out the combination locks—taking special note of who has the one with the combination you've memorized.

Ask the kids to open the combination locks—but instead of giving them the correct combinations, ask them to try some of the following methods.

- Try some of their favorite numbers.
- Roll the dice three times and use those numbers.
- Ask someone in the room to suggest a set of three numbers that they like.

Obviously, none of those solutions will work. If you want to have a little more fun with them, ask one of the kids to hand you their lock (the one you know the combination for). Ask them to give you the same three numbers they were trying—unsuccessfully. Instead of using those numbers, dial in the combination you memorized. Open the lock and hand it back to them.

- Tell the kids to try harder.
- Tell them to believe they can do it.
- Tell them that you'll buy them a pizza if they can get the lock open with one more try.

Again, nothing will work. Don't draw this out for too long or the kids will get frustrated.

Teaching the Lesson

Trying to open the lock was frustrating. We all know that to open a combination lock properly (not by cutting it), we need the right combination. That is absolutely true, right? Most rational people would agree with that.

We live in a world where many say there is no absolute truth.

They say there is "your truth" or "my truth" . . . but they don't believe there can be universal, absolute truth that is the same for everybody in the whole world.

Yes, we have "preferences" that differ. My favorite meal is spaghetti—that is absolutely true. Your favorite meal may be steak—and that could be absolutely true for you. But we must not make the mistake of thinking that absolute truth—something that is absolutely true for every person in the world—no longer exists.

If there is no absolute truth, where does the Bible fit in?

Once we start buying in to the lie that there is no absolute truth for every person in the world, we weaken the potential impact of the Bible in our lives. If we do not believe the Bible is our source of absolute moral truth, we lose our compass in life. The devil and his demons know that, which is why they want us to doubt any absolute truth exists.

Science, math, and our entire universe is full of evidence of absolute truth.

- Water freezes at 32 degrees Fahrenheit and boils at 212 degrees Fahrenheit at sea level. That's true if you live here or in France.
- Drop a bowling ball from your roof—and it will fall. Gravity is a universal, absolute truth for all people, all over the world.
- North is north, no matter where you live.
- A true pound or kilogram weighs the same no matter who weighs it or where on earth they are.
- A true meter is the same length . . . all over the world. It's not a matter of opinion. There's not *your meter* or *my meter*.
- Oil and water have different densities, so they will separate.
- Time is universal. One hour is one hour, no matter where you live.
- There are laws of buoyancy. A rubber ball will float in water whether it's in the Atlantic Ocean, the Pacific Ocean, the Amazon River, or the Mississippi River.
- Seasons. Spring follows winter . . . all over the world.
- Even our solar system runs on absolute truth. If it didn't, we'd either *freeze to death* or *burn up*.
- Put your thumb on a table and let a volunteer hit your thumb with a hammer, and you'll find the absolute truth that *it will hurt*. Demo that anywhere in the world, and you'll come up with the same absolute truth.
- There are laws of thermodynamics: heat transfers. Put your hand on a hot stove and heat will transfer . . . no matter how much you don't want it to.
- Absolute truth *governs our universe*.

So those who say absolute truth doesn't exist are *absolutely wrong*. Science—and our entire universe—proves that.

If these people are wrong about the existence of absolute truth in the universe, isn't it likely they're also wrong in their claims that the Bible holds no absolute truth?

As Christians, we need to understand that the Bible is our source of absolute truth.

- The Bible is the source of truth as to how to have a relationship with God.
- The Bible is the source of truth as to how to get to heaven.
- The Bible is the source of moral truth . . . of what is right and wrong for all humankind.
- The Bible is the source of truth of how to live a life that is fulfilling—and that counts for eternity.

Jesus came to bring us truth.

Dozens and dozens of times in the Gospels we read a verse with Jesus saying, "I tell you the truth." Let me read you some references: Matthew 5:18; 5:26; 6:2; 6:5; 6:16; 8:10; 10:15; 10:23; 10:42; 11:11; 13:17; 16:28; 17:20; 18:3; 18:13; 18:18; 19:23; 19:28; 21:21; 21:31; 23:36; 24:2; 24:34; 24:47; 25:12; 26:13; 26:21; 26:34—and these only represent the Gospel of Matthew.

When Jesus was questioned by Pilate, he said this:

You say that I am a king. In fact, the reason I was born and came into the world is to testify to the truth. Everyone on the side of truth listens to me. (John 18:37)

One of Jesus's express purposes was to teach truth. Over and over, Scripture records Jesus

- Straightening out misconceptions about God
- Straightening out misconceptions about Scripture

We live in a world of lies. And one of those lies is that there is no absolute truth.

Summing It Up

Many people don't want to believe there is absolute truth, because then they'd have to live according to what the Bible says.

- They want to live how they feel like living.
- They want to believe they can live however they want—and still get to heaven. They reason that a good, loving God can't possibly have only one way to get to heaven.

Let's look at that issue of getting to heaven for just a moment.

We all understand that there's only one proper way to open a combination lock . . . one correct sequence of numbers. A combination lock is often used to protect a shed, a locker, or a bike. Why is it that some people have such a hard time believing God would have only one way to get into heaven—something infinitely more valuable than the things we protect with a combination lock? People listen to friends as to how one gets to heaven. They roll the dice, in a sense, gambling with their own theories. But truth is truth. You can't change it by believing or trying harder.

If the Bible is our source of truth—and we live in a world of lies—doesn't it make sense to read the Word daily?

Reading the Bible daily—and putting what we read into practice—is the best way to avoid traps in life and to avoid getting deceived by the world's lies. And that's the absolute truth.

Let's pray that God will open our eyes and help us understand and live by his truth daily.

> Open my eyes that I may see
> wonderful things in your law. (Ps. 119:18)

6

Secret Message

THEME: The real you behind the façade . . . especially when the heat is on

KEEP IT SAFE

You'll be using an open flame for this lesson. Use proper safety precautions.

THINGS YOU'LL NEED

☐ Milk

☐ One raw egg

☐ Lemon juice (the concentrated type used for cooking)

☐ Orange juice and/or apple juice

☐ One sheet of 8.5 x 11 paper for each person in the group

- ☐ Cotton swabs (such as the Q-Tip brand)
- ☐ Handheld hairdryer (or you could use a small electric fan)
- ☐ Lighter or a candle on a stand (and matches)
- ☐ Common sense—you'll be using an open flame here
- ☐ Quick access to water in case the flame gets out of control (have a filled bucket nearby, do the activity over a sink with running water, or go outdoors by a running hose)

Advance Prep

As always, it's best to test the object lesson out before you do it with the kids. And when you get to the part where you're using fire, be sure to do this outside, with a bucket of water or running hose handy, or over the kitchen sink.

- Dip a cotton swab in milk and write something on the paper. Apply it somewhat sparingly, because the liquid must dry before you'll be able to make it appear with the flame.
- Use a fresh swab and do the same with the lemon juice and apple or orange juice. You may want to label the spots so you remember which liquid you used where.
- Crack the egg, separate it, and use just the egg white for secret ink.
- Mix a solution of equal parts milk and lemon juice and write with that. Out of all the liquids I tested, I found this last mix seemed to work the best for easy readability once the flame was applied.
- Dry each of the sample writings using a hairdryer or fan.
- When the paper is dry, position it so you can bring the flame from your lighter or the candle close. I had to practically touch the paper with the flame before the words appeared—but you don't want to touch the paper. **I did this over the kitchen sink and kept the water running, which was a good thing because I started the paper on fire— twice.** With just a bit of practice you'll be able to make the words appear without setting the paper on fire at all!

Running the Activity

Explain to the kids how you'd like each of them to write a secret message on a piece of paper using the various liquids—just like you did when you practiced this in advance. Likely they'll write only one word with each of the different liquids.

Once they're done, get them busy drying the paper with the fan or hairdryer.

After all the papers are dry, use the flame source to "reveal" the secret messages. A word of caution here: depending on the ages of the kids, likely you're the only one who will handle the candle or lighter. Carefully pick the location you plan to do this. Use extreme caution.

Teaching the Lesson

- How visible was the writing before you put the flame to it?
- If you tried different solutions, which one seemed to give you the clearest message?

The flame burns the carbon in each solution (milk, egg white, juice) before it burns the paper, making the hidden messages appear. In real life, there are times we feel the "heat" from all sorts of things. Trouble. Problems with friends. Bullies. Homework. Tests. Temptation. Sin.

When we applied the heat to the secret writing, the flame revealed the hidden words. When we're feeling the heat in some area of life, what might it reveal in us that probably would have stayed hidden otherwise?

Heat	Revealed
being tired	crabbiness comes out
being busy	self-absorbed and oblivious to others
embarrassed	put someone else down
homework not done	cheat . . . copy a friend's paper
confronted with doing something wrong	lie to cover it

Heat	Revealed
feeling tempted in some way	secretly satisfy it
being wronged in some way	anger—aka pride

When the heat is on, often we feel pressure to react in a way that isn't good. Does the "heat" situation *force* us to do something bad, or does the situation *reveal* what is really inside us? Listen to what Jesus says about the things we say.

> For what is in your heart determines what you say. A good person produces good things from the treasury of a good heart, and an evil person produces evil things from the treasury of an evil heart. (Matt. 12:34–35)

What does this Scripture tell us is the source of the nasty things we say? Is it simply that we're having a bad day? The truth is hardships often reveal our character. Like the flame did to the hidden writing on the paper, the "heat" of hardships shows us what's really in our hearts.

If I choose to cheat on a test because I don't know the answer, what does that say about my character?

In Joshua 7, we read the sad story of a man named Achan. When he and the other Israelites fought and defeated Jericho, Achan saw treasure in the enemy city and it revealed his secret desires. Achan stole some of the plunder and hid it in his tent.

God saw what Achan did and exposed him. Achan confessed to Joshua, explaining his actions in Joshua 7:21. "I wanted them so much that I took them" (NLT). When the temptation was in front of him and nobody was around to see, his secret desires and lust appeared. Does this sound familiar?

Let me read you another verse.

> And so the LORD says,
>   "These people say they are mine.
> They honor me with their lips,
>   but their hearts are far from me." (Isa. 29:13 NLT)

We can call ourselves Christians, followers of Christ—that's part of honoring God with our *lips*—but when the heat is on, what do our actions reveal about our *hearts*?

Summing It Up

When the heat is on, what kind of messages are we sending others about our Christian identity? About the difference Christ makes in our lives?

- If we talk one way and live another, what message are we really sending?
- If we talk about loving others, and our actions show it's really "all about me," or we ridicule and make fun of others, what attraction is there for them to become Christians?
- Besides affecting others, or how others see Christians, how do the secret messages that come out of us when we face heat affect *us*?

Let's ask the Holy Spirit to reveal these inconsistencies. Then be willing to work at them and ask God to help change us. To forgive us and to make us into the kind of people who don't have "secret messages" that are contrary to what a Christian's character should be.

The Lord wants us to have a character that is consistent with what a Christian should be.

The truth is that as our character becomes more and more like Christ's, the benefits to us are immeasurably high. Can you think of some ways this may make life better for you?

Take this secret message you wrote and tape it up in your room so you see it. Let it be a reminder to ask God to change your heart and your character so that any message that comes out of you when the heat is on is totally consistent with being a Christian.

Take a Stab at Kindness

THEME: Talking kindly to and about others

THINGS YOU'LL NEED

- [ ] Gallon-size plastic food storage bag
- [ ] Small rocks, marbles, or something similar—enough to fill about half of the plastic storage bag. *Important:* you're going to poke holes in the bag, and you don't want any of the rocks or marbles to slip out. So be careful not to use something too small. I used smooth river rock that I picked up at a pet store (for aquariums). Being a little bigger, the stones worked especially well.
- [ ] One or two small, sharp objects with which to puncture the bag. I find a nail or scratch awl works best. The hole is big enough to let water out of the bag without the marbles or rocks slipping out.
- [ ] Pitcher of water
- [ ] Box of standard adhesive bandages
- [ ] Towels for cleanup

Advance Prep

This lesson is really easy, but you'll want to test it out ahead of time.

- Fill the storage bag about half full of rocks.
- Poke some holes in sides and bottom of the plastic bag with the nail or scratch awl. Plenty of holes is best—but not so many that you lose any of the rocks inside the bag.
- Now grab a full pitcher of water and pour it into the bag. A second person is advisable here. One holds the bag, the other pours. The bag should spout fountains of water all over the place. Perfect.

Running the Activity

Carefully pick the spot where you intend to do this with the kids. If all goes well, you'll have a bit of a flood. Keep the pitcher of water out of sight.

Invite the kids to take turns using the nail or awl to poke holes in the bag of rocks. Remember—take the bag back before any of its contents actually drop out of the bag.

Now hold the bag up and ask the kids some questions.

- It felt kind of good to stab the bag like that, didn't it?
- Even with all that stabbing, how many rocks did we lose? None, right? The bag is still holding all the rocks just fine, right?

Let's see what kind of shape this bag is *really* in. I'd like one of you to hold the bag open with both hands. (Once they do, pour water in from the pitcher. If you want to be kind, have them stand. If not, have them sit and hold the bag over their lap while you pour. Water will spout all over, so you may want to have a bucket nearby to drop the bag of rocks into.) Be sure to have a towel handy.

Okay, so it didn't *look* like we did all that much damage at first, but in reality, we made a pretty good mess of the bag, didn't we?

Teaching the Lesson

- Can any of you share a time you really were hurt by something somebody said to or about you? It could have been me, a friend, a coach, a teacher, or maybe some kid who you can't stand. How did you feel?
- Did you show how much it affected you, or did you try to cover it up by ignoring the comment or laughing it off?
- So, in reality, even though we may not act like the comments had a lasting effect, they did. Do I have that right?

Sometimes we're like this bag of rocks. We look like we're holding it all together, but in reality, we're full of holes. The hurtful things people say cause damage.

- Is it possible that *we* do the same things to others?
- Is it possible that we make hurtful, unkind comments to others, and they cover it up with a laugh or by seeming to ignore it just so we don't know how much our comment hurt them?

Why do we say things that hurt others? Sure, sometimes we don't realize when we say something unkind, but other times we *want* to hurt that person. Or we want to make ourselves look better by putting someone else down. Sometimes we say something nasty to pay them back for something they said or did to us. Listen to this verse.

If you claim to be religious but don't control your tongue, you are fooling yourself, and your religion is worthless. (James 1:26 NLT)

What does this verse say about your Christianity if you're careless with how you talk? Where do you find it particularly hard to watch what you say? Listen to another verse.

Watch your tongue and keep your mouth shut,
and you will stay out of trouble. (Prov. 21:23 NLT)

All right, let's try something. Take this box of bandages and patch up the holes. (Give them a chance to work at this.)

Even if you put a bandage over every one of these holes, the bag will likely still leak—and it will look like a mess.

It's the same with trying to patch up the damage we do when we say something mean to someone else. It's very, very hard to fix the wounds we inflict with our tongues.

Kids, we've all experienced the pain or embarrassment of something said to us that was unkind, rude, or insensitive. Let's make sure *we* aren't doing the same to others.

- As Christians, the things we say and do should be kind.
- When we're kind with the things we say, we keep ourselves from trouble.

Let's take a look at a great verse in Proverbs.

> Some people make cutting remarks,
>> but the words of the wise bring healing. (12:18 NLT)

According to this verse, the person who watches what they say is *wise*, and the things they say actually *help* other people. Their words encourage others.

- Does that sound like the kind of people we want to be, with God's help?
- How can we do that at home? With friends? At school? At church?

Summing It Up

Let me read you a verse from Ephesians.

> Don't use foul or abusive language. Let everything you say be good and helpful, so that your words will be an encouragement to those who hear them. (4:29 NLT)

Wouldn't that be a great thing, to be known as one who encourages and helps others rather than one who carelessly hurts people by the things they say?

I'd like each of you to take one of these rocks. Stick it in your backpack, a drawer, or your pocket. And every time you see it, remember to watch what you say. *The words of the wise bring healing.*

Slip-Sliding Away

THEME: Run from temptation . . . before you get on the slippery slope and can't stop

THINGS YOU'LL NEED

☐ A roll of plastic sheeting approximately 10 x 25 feet. Pick this up at the hardware store, often in the paint section. Get the thick stuff, at least 3 mils thick.

☐ Liquid dish soap . . . a full bottle

☐ Water hose

☐ At least two tent stakes (or weights to hold the plastic in place)

☐ Broom, mop, or rag to spread the liquid soap on the plastic

Advance Prep

The idea here is to make an outdoor slip 'n' slide for the kids. Unroll the plastic sheeting to its full twenty-five-foot length, but keep it doubled up width-wise so you have extra thickness. If your kids are younger, you can double-up the length too, making it only twelve feet long.

You'll want the kids to get in swimsuits for this one. While they're getting changed, you can be setting up the slide, or have them help you after they're done. With this devotional, either way works.

Once the plastic is in place, stake down the two corners at the start so it won't buckle when the kids run and slide on it. Pace off a good twenty feet or so before the start of the slide and put a marker there for a starting line. You want the kids to have a good running start so they're up to full speed before hitting the slide.

Next, use the hose and get the entire slide wet. Squirt on an excessive amount of liquid dish soap and use a broom, mop, or rag to be sure you've covered the surface of the plastic sheeting so that every inch is soapy . . . and slippery.

Running the Activity

Each of the kids, individually, will get a running start. Their goal is to slide the entire length of the plastic without tobogganing off either side.

Give each of the kids one turn on the slide and have them line up again. Reapply water and liquid soap as needed.

Now you'll have them run and slide again, but this time you'll do it a little differently. Tell them that you may say "stop" after they start sliding—and their goal will change. If you yell "stop," they're to try to come to a complete stop before reaching the end of the slide.

You want this to be as close to impossible for them to stop as you can make it. To help toward that end, be sure the kids are still running at the slide at full speed. Also, wait until they're at least halfway down the slide before you tell them to stop.

Teaching the Lesson

Once you started sliding, it was really hard to stop, right? If there had been a cliff at the end of that slip 'n' slide, I'm afraid all of you would have sailed right over the edge. And this illustrates a truth about life that I want to remind you about.

Temptation can be kind of a "slippery slope," as some call it. Sometimes there are things that we'd like to do that deep down we know are wrong. We know God wouldn't want us to do them. But instead of staying away from those things, we let our minds go there.

- We think about it.
- We think about what it would be like to do that wrong thing.
- We think about how we could get away with it without anybody knowing.
- Sometimes we try to get really close to the temptation.
- We want to see what it is all about.

In a way, we end up tempting ourselves. Listen to what God's Word says.

When tempted, no one should say, "God is tempting me." For God cannot be tempted by evil, nor does he tempt anyone; but each one is tempted when they are dragged away by their own evil desire and enticed. Then, after desire has conceived, it gives birth to sin; and sin, when it is full-grown, gives birth to death. (James 1:13–15)

According to these verses, we get *ourselves* in trouble because of how much we want things that are wrong. It's like we're running toward that wrong thing, at least in our minds. When that happens, and an opportunity to do that wrong thing comes along . . . it can be really, really hard to stop.

Often when people talk about temptation, they quote this verse:

No temptation has overtaken you except what is common to mankind. And God is faithful; he will not let you be tempted beyond what you can bear. But when you are tempted, he will also provide a way out so that you can endure it. (1 Cor. 10:13)

The things that tempt you are not new or unique to you. Lots of people have been tempted in the same way. But God is good. He always provides a way out. A way to say no.

Remember when you were running for the slip 'n' slide, and I yelled "stop" after you were already sliding? It was a little late, right? What if I had yelled "stop" before you got to the plastic? You could have stopped then, right?

God does the same thing. He warns you *before* you get near the temptation. Often, that is your time to escape, not when you're in the middle of it. Remember the story of Joseph when he was a slave in Egypt? His master's wife tried to tempt him to sin against God, and what did Joseph do?

Joseph ran. He ran right out of the house. He got out of there before the temptation could grab him and drag him down. I'm convinced that if he hadn't run, he may not have left at all. Sometimes we need to do that. *We must run away from sin, not toward it.*

Summing It Up

Imagine the slip 'n' slide was positioned at the edge of a cliff. The way you were zipping across it, you'd have all gone over that cliff once you were sliding, right? Temptation is just like that. If we don't run from temptation when God gives us the chance, we'll probably slide right into sin. And there's always a cliff we go over after we sin, isn't there? There's a price to be paid. There's regret and hurt. There are often consequences—like punishment and loss of trust.

The slide was fun. If there was a real cliff, it wouldn't end so well. That's the way it is when we get too close to temptation. The wrong thing we want to do can be fun, but it is really, really hard to stop. And it always ends up badly.

Let's pray that God helps us to run from temptation, not toward it.

Safety Line

THEME: Understanding how the "fear of the Lord" keeps us safe

THINGS YOU'LL NEED

See the Advance Prep section. There are no supplies needed for this one, but you'll need to do a little research.

Advance Prep

You'll want to find a place you can take the kids where there is some activity they'll do that requires a safety line or harness.

- Any kind of a zip line or ropes course would be perfect.
- Any type of a climbing wall will work just as well, although it does require more athletic ability.

If none of the above is a possibility, you could take a trip to a theme park where there are rides with a safety harness or collar that keeps riders from unplanned exits.

But first do an online search for *zip line* or *climbing wall* with your city or zip code tacked on the end, and you should have plenty to choose from.

Because you'll be traveling to a different location, this lesson will monopolize a bigger chunk of time than most of the other lessons in this book. That's totally fine, as long as the activity is good.

After you've done your research and selected a place, announce it to the family. "Hey, next Saturday for family devotions we're going to a zip line park." That will raise anticipation for the event, which means they'll likely remember the lesson you teach just that much longer.

Running the Activity

Enjoy the zip line, ropes course, climbing wall, or theme park with the kids. You won't be doing any teaching or applications until the drive home. But there are two things you can do earlier in the day, while you're doing the activity, to set things up nicely for the talk.

- Remind them to check the safety line or harness just before they launch or start climbing.
- Take a picture of each of the kids while they're hooked to the safety line or in the harness. This would be a great thing to print up for them later . . . as a reminder of what they learned in this lesson.

Teaching the Lesson

On the drive home, talk with the kids about the fun they had. And if you can stop at a fast-food place for some kind of snack for the kids, that would be a great idea. Actually, go inside rather than eating in the car while you drive. You'll be able to face your kids that way, and they'll have a snack to keep them busy while you ask them the following questions.

- Did anybody feel that the safety line (or strap, bar, harness) was a pain or a bother?
- Did anybody feel like they'd have rather gone without it?
- The safety line was a really, really important and essential part of enjoying the fun. Without it, this whole thing would have been a lot more dangerous. That line ensured that you wouldn't get off track somehow and get hurt. Do any of you think I'd have let you do it *without* the safety line?
- Do you think that there are guidelines and limits I place on you as a parent to keep you safe? To keep you from some dangerous course of action? Can you think of any of them?
- In the Christian life, there are things that work like a safety line or harness to keep us on course too. How does the truth of the Bible work like a safety line? How does the Holy Spirit work like a safety harness?

There's one safety line or harness that God talks about in the Bible that few think about. It's referred to as the "fear of the Lord." It is a healthy fear. A good fear. It is about having a strong respect for God—not just as a God of love but as a God of justice. It is knowing that even though God loves and forgives, God is also just. He must punish us when we do wrong. There are consequences.

- How might knowing that we can't hide anything we do, say, or think from God actually be like a safety harness . . . keeping us safe?
- How might knowing that we can't get away with sinning because God will deal with our sin actually be like a safety line . . . protecting us?

Consider what this verse means.

Do not be deceived: God cannot be mocked. A man reaps what he sows. Whoever sows to please their flesh, from the flesh will reap destruction; whoever sows to please the Spirit, from the Spirit will reap eternal life. Let us not become weary in doing good, for at the proper time we will reap a harvest if we do not give up. (Gal. 6:7–9)

"Do not be deceived." We live in a world of deception—and it has certainly oozed into the church. Some see God as being only about love—and they forget he is also a God of justice. When that happens, people tend to be selective with how they obey God's Word. They tend to ignore many principles for living that God gives us.

- When we do things or live in ways that conflict with God's Word—thinking he won't notice somehow—how is that like we're mocking God?
- According to Galatians 6:7–9, how scary are the consequences of living how we want—rather than in obedience to God's Word?

This sense of fear—of knowing God will deal with our sin—is part of what it means to *fear the Lord*. And fearing the Lord is also about having a deep sense of reverence and awe for God—enough to honor him with obedience. This fear and reverence work like a safety line to keep us from the danger and regret of sin. Make sense?

Living with a healthy "fear of the Lord" is a wise thing to do. Proverbs 1:7 describes the fear of the Lord as the beginning of knowledge. How is it really wise to have that healthy fear of God's justice?

Some people might tell you that fearing the Lord is an Old Testament thing, but they're missing something important. This healthy fear of and reverence for God was a huge factor in the growth of the early New Testament church. In Acts 5, we read the story of Ananias and Sapphira, a couple who were dishonest and paid with their lives. Acts 5:5 and 5:11 tell us that after God's judgment on them, "great fear seized" the church and all who heard about it.

The Christians in the early church had been basking in God's love, and the incident with Ananias and his wife reminded everyone that God would not wink at sin. It was a wake-up call for the early church. It was a reminder to be careful to obey God's Word and not to get sloppy. So a type of fear gripped them. It was a fear that helped keep the early church believers in line. It kept them from falling into sin. It kept them safe.

Fear of the Lord was an essential element of the early church, as God made clear when he summed up the church.

Then the church throughout Judea, Galilee and Samaria enjoyed a time of peace and was strengthened. *Living in the fear of the Lord* and encouraged by the Holy Spirit, it increased in numbers. (Acts 9:31, emphasis added)

In our age, we see more and more churches and believers growing relaxed in their obedience to God's Word. They capitalize on God's love—forgetting that the best way to show their love for him is by their obedience.

I want you to know the whole truth, not just part of it. I want you to stay on the right paths. To stay safe. To stay dedicated to God. That is part of what the Holy Spirit and the fear of the Lord do for us.

Summing It Up

The safety line wasn't designed to *restrict* your fun. It kept you safe so that you could enjoy the fun. It was a way to ensure you wouldn't fall and get hurt.

Obeying God's Word and having a healthy fear *of* God and reverence *for* God will do the same for us. These won't restrict us so much as they let us enjoy all the good things God has for us. A healthy fear of and reverence for our God keeps us from the consequences of sin and pain of regret.

The ride we took today was a lot of fun. But it wouldn't be fun if we were in an ambulance right now. Thank God for safety lines and harnesses. And let's thank him for the safety line of a healthy fear of and respect for God that keep us from falling into sin and keep us safe on the ride of life.

Lights Out

THEME: Finding God's will for your life

THINGS YOU'LL NEED

☐ $5 bill for each of the kids. If you want to go with a higher denomination, that would be fantastic. Just go with whatever you can afford. You won't be getting the money back after the devotional. Label each bill with the name of one of your kids.

☐ A flashlight (or use the one on your phone)

☐ Ideally, some kind of snack to share while you tie this together

Advance Prep

Plan to do this one at night, or in a basement or other room you can make completely dark. Hide a $5 bill for each of the kids just before your family devotional time. Be sure the money is hidden high and completely out of their reach. If you've got teenagers, you may be taping the money to the ceiling. Your goal is to make sure they don't find the money—not until you help them, anyway.

Running the Activity

Explain to the kids that there is a $5 bill for each of them in the darkened room and that you'll give them a couple of minutes to find it—in the dark. If you have teenagers, confiscate their phones before they go in—otherwise they'll use their flashlight app or the glow from the screen. Send the kids in one at a time or all together. Either way works. Just don't let this part go too long. In the dark, a full minute seems like five.

After the time is up, offer to help them find their hidden money—with your flashlight. Lead each one to their $5 bill and, because it is out of reach, reach for it yourself and hand it to them. They may feel you cheated because you brought a flashlight. That's fine. You can use that later. But they shouldn't complain much . . . they get to keep the $5.

After each of them has their cash, maybe grab a snack and talk about the lesson behind this.

Teaching the Lesson

Sometimes trying to figure out God's will for your life, or for some decision you're facing, can seem as impossible as finding that $5 bill in a dark room. How much easier was it when we went in together to find the money—especially with the flashlight?

Finding God's will doesn't have to be quite the mystery we sometimes make it out to be. Sometimes it's obvious. Like how the Bible tells us in Philippians 2:14 that we should do all things without complaining and arguing. That's God's will: don't complain and argue when things aren't going your way. The hard thing is *doing* God's will, right?

Other times finding God's will requires a little help—like the way I helped you find the $5. That's one reason God gives us parents.

Sometimes it's hard to take Mom's or Dad's advice. I get that. You have something inside you that wants to be free. And you'll get your freedom. It's coming. But our job is to get you there in one piece. To help you develop into the kind of person who has good character and integrity. One who makes wise choices.

We love you and we've had a lot of experience in life. This often brings wisdom—exactly what is needed to steer you in the right direction.

Many times you've heard people tell you things like "You can do anything you want to in life—you can become anything you really want to be." That's a nice thought, but the important thing is knowing and doing what *God* plans for you to do in life—and Ephesians 2:10 makes it clear that he has plans for us.

So how do we find God's will . . . his big and little plans for us? Let me read you two verses that hold the key.

> Therefore, I urge you brothers and sisters, in view of God's mercy, to offer your bodies as a living sacrifice, wholly and pleasing to God—this is your true and proper worship. Do not conform to the pattern of this world, but be transformed by the renewing of your mind. *Then* you will be able to test and approve what God's will is—his good, pleasing, and perfect will. (Rom. 12:1–2, emphasis added)

- When we offer our bodies as living sacrifices, it's not about climbing up on an altar. What is this Scripture talking about?

- Offering ourselves to God or surrendering to him—and living in a way that pleases him—is referred to as our "spiritual act of worship" in these verses. Clearly, the kind of worship God wants from us goes beyond singing worship songs. What might that look like?

- As we surrender to him and live in obedience to his Word instead of the way the world lives, something happens. Notice the word *then* in the passage. It says *then* we will be able to "test and approve what God's will is." When is *then*?

- So, according to these verses, we need to surrender to God. We need to obey his Word in the big and little things. We do this with a spirit of gratitude for the mercy he's shown us. And as we do that, we will find God's will. We'll be able to test it. We'll be able to check it out. Take it for a test drive. And what does the passage say we'll find out about God's will for us, as far as how we'll like it?

Summing It Up

Finding God's will in big and little things doesn't have to leave you in the dark. God gave you parents to help you. And he gave us his Word. As we surrender, and as we obey his Word with gratitude, he will lead us to the very things he's designed us to do and become. Good things.

The $5 bill wasn't much, but it's just to remind you that finding and doing God's will come with rewards . . . and those rewards are priceless.

One more thing. The $5 bill was out of reach. You needed a little help to get it, right? Often, that's exactly the way it is with God's will. The direction he wants you to go—let's say it is forgiving someone who wronged you—may seem out of reach. He doesn't expect you to reach it alone. You have us to help you, and ultimately God will help you do it as you ask him to. Why would he want us to do only what we could do without his help?

House of the Dead

THEME: The danger of pornography—and deliverance from it

+12 THINGS YOU'LL NEED

☐ Select a local funeral home to visit

A Special Word for Parents

Because of the nature of this topic, you'll need to decide when this is right for your kids. But your kids will likely be exposed to an opportunity to view pornography at a younger age than you'd expect—so you need to prepare them. Also, don't delay talking to the older kids about this simply because of the younger ones. Take the older ones aside and teach this lesson if you need to.

Advance Prep

Contact a local funeral home director and arrange a visit. Explain the purpose of your visit by saying something like this: "I'm talking to my kids about basic truths of life and death. I'm wondering if I can come with my kids and get a quick walk through your facility. I'd just like them to see one of the parlors and hopefully the room where you display caskets for sale. Would that be possible? I'll be using the visit as a reference point to talk to them more after we leave."

If the director says no, keep looking. You'll find one who will agree to the little tour. You're really not asking for much here. It's not like you're asking to see where they do the embalming . . . although that would make a fantastic addition to your tour if they are open to it and your kids are the right ages.

I know . . . going to a funeral home is a creepy activity. I totally agree. I hate funeral homes. But don't shortcut this and simply *talk* about a funeral home, even if the kids have all been there before. This time it will be different because they aren't going to see anyone; they're going to see the funeral home itself. The power is in the visual. The activity. The actual visit through that place that smells of funeral flowers and, somehow, death. There is something as unnatural about a funeral home as a body displayed in a casket. Perfectly manicured. Everything in its place. And somehow so devoid of life that you can't wait to get out of there.

The kids need to *feel* this so that the lesson you teach them has maximum impact. You want the kids to be uncomfortable with this little visit. You want them creeped out just a bit.

You're going to talk to them about the dangers of pornography . . . and how to break free. Now, the enemy of your soul is going to whisper something to you right now. *Who are you to teach the kids about this? You know what you've done. You know what you're still doing.* Look, according to the statistics, most men and many women have seen pornography. Don't let the fact that you've seen it make you feel disqualified to help your kids. The enemy wants to keep you from warning and protecting them. Don't let the enemy dupe you into neglecting your duty.

And, men, if you're struggling with pornography, I want to suggest you pick up my book *Super Husband, Super Dad*. The tagline is "You can be the hero your family needs." The book is unlike any other men's book you've read. Read the whole book. It is so important. In it I share so many things that you need to know now, before your kids are gone.

And especially read chapter 13, "Frankenstein, Dracula, and the Curse of the Wolfman," starting on page 105. I talk about how pornography is a monster and how to truly break free. You'll get a lot more practical help and insight on the topic than I can convey in this devotional.

Running the Activity

Prep the kids before you enter the funeral home. Tell them you're just going to walk through together. Ask them to observe what they can. Ask them to try to notice what they feel or smell. Any impressions they get. Let them know that you'll talk about their observations afterward.

If the director walks you through, thank him or her afterward, and consider going to a fast-food place to debrief a bit instead of going home to do that.

Teaching the Lesson

- A funeral home is not a place I like to visit. It's a place of the dead and a place where the dead are mourned. How many of you feel the same way?
- What did you feel? Hear? Smell? What impressions did you have?

The Bible talks of another "house of the dead." It warns that the house of an adulterer, or prostitute, is a place of death. Before we actually look at some Bible verses, let's go over a few definitions.

- A person who has sex outside of marriage is an adulterer or adulteress (male or female).
- One who has sex in exchange for some form of payment is a prostitute.
- A man or woman being filmed or photographed naked or having sex is not simply an actor or actress. If they are doing it for pay, they are a prostitute. If they are doing it for free, they are an adulterer or adulteress.
- A person who views pornography is in a very real sense going to the house of a prostitute/adulterer/adulteress. At the very least, they are looking in the window.

Listen to what the Bible says.

> Now then, my sons, listen to me;
>> pay attention to what I say.
> Do not let your heart turn to her ways
>> or stray into her paths.
> Many are the victims she has brought down;
>> her slain are a mighty throng.
> Her house is a highway to the grave,
>> leading down to the chambers of death. (Prov. 7:24–27)

- How can you tell the urgency of this issue by how the first verse begins?
- When people stray and get involved watching pornography, where does the straying start—before even one physical step is taken down that path?
- According to these verses, how many people become victims *themselves* when they stray down the path of pornography . . . viewing adulterers, adulteresses, and prostitutes? Is it many people or few?
- Becoming a victim means there is a death that follows. What types of death might God be talking about, besides physical death?
- The verses describe that there isn't simply a little path to this house of death but rather a highway. What does that suggest about the ease of getting there, the speed of getting there, and the number of people who will travel that route?
- How might that tie in with Matthew 7:13? Jesus said, "Enter through the narrow gate. For wide is the gate and broad is the road that leads to destruction, and many enter through it."

A Special Word for Parents

There are many more verses I could share, but the passage above covers what we really need to hit for this one. If you have a son or daughter who doesn't believe pornography is really wrong, or that the Bible doesn't speak to it, please read chapter 13 of *Super Husband, Super Dad* and you'll get a lot more ammo.

Pornography will hurt you. Change you. If you continue on the path to her house, death of some sort always follows.

- Death of innocence
- Death of purity
- Death of dreams
- Death of God's best plans for you
- Death of integrity
- Death of self-respect
- Death of future happiness
- Death of future satisfying sex with your spouse

And the list goes on. Pornography is a trap. It offers pleasure and thrills, but in the end it brings death. I want to urge you to avoid it, in all its forms. Understand what pornography really is . . . a house of death.

Can you imagine going to that funeral home, alone, at night? And then finding out you can't get out? That you're locked in?

Getting involved in watching pornography can be like getting locked inside a funeral home. Pornography can be as addicting as cocaine. And the effects of pornography are devastating. I want to encourage you to avoid it at all costs.

You will be tempted. You will have opportunities. But you must steer clear, because pornography is all about the enemy taking good sex that God created for marriage and offering you a way to experience some of the wonder of it early. But by doing so you end up on a very dangerous highway that has taken down many, many strong and good people. The road leads to all kinds of death. Often, continuing to be involved in pornography will hurt your relationship with your spouse someday. That seems like a long way off. But you must protect yourself now so that you can truly enjoy all God has for you later.

If your kids are in their teens, chances are high that they've seen pornography, and if so, they may already have difficulty stopping. You'll need to talk about that more with them. If they tell you that is the case, or you sense it may be so, you'll want to take your son or daughter off to the side and address it. Again, pick up *Super Husband, Super Dad*. Read chapter 13. See what you'd like to add from that book—maybe just for your older kids. Many sources talk about "accountability"

A Special Word for Parents

The following is optional. If one of your kids is involved in pornography and wants to break free, here are some starting points.

1. You'll need to confess and repent. Viewing pornography is wrong.
2. You'll need Holy Spirit–control . . . the Holy Spirit can help change your heart and give you different desires. You'll need to ask him to do that. And it isn't a one-time prayer. This is something you'll need to do regularly.
3. You'll need to exercise self-control. You'll need to say no and get rid of the easy ways you're accessing pornography. If that means dumping the smartphone, then do it. Jesus talks about aggressively attacking the lack of self-control in Matthew 5:29–30. God will help you with self-control if you ask him.
4. You'll need to stay in the Word. Daily. It is our source of truth in a world of lies. Our source of strength in areas we feel weak.
5. You'll need some sort of accountability. This is good but by no means as powerful as numbers one through four above. Mom or Dad can be that accountability partner for you. But remember, ultimately accountability needs to come from within . . . from heart change.

as if that is *the* answer to breaking free from the rigor mortis grip of pornography. It is not. Accountability is only a very small part of truly breaking free. Your kids need much more than accountability. They need a change of heart—and that is the type of thing that God does so well.

Obviously, we've only hit this topic lightly. But keep watching the kids. Check their computer and phone history. Be very careful about time spent at the homes of friends—especially overnighters. And if one of the kids is having a problem viewing / breaking free from pornography, you need to help them get past this.

Summing It Up

A funeral home is a creepy place to be. It definitely isn't someplace we'd want to hang out to have a good time. And we need that same sense of avoidance when it comes to going to the "house of the dead" mentioned in Proverbs. Pornography is dangerous. Deadly. Nobody can "handle it." There's always a terribly high cost—and likely it will be more evident in your future than it is now.

Think of pornography as being the house of the dead. Avoid it. You don't want to get trapped there any more than you'd want to be locked in a funeral home. The dead are there. And you don't want to join them in any way.

> Whoever strays from the path of prudence
>   comes to rest in the company of the dead. (Prov. 21:16)

If you're having a problem with pornography—and you know you need to break free—talk to me. I want to help you get past this.

Well Done

THEME: When life is bad, remember God may be making you into someone better

THINGS YOU'LL NEED

- ☐ Hamburger patties, buns, condiments . . . everything needed to grill burgers
- ☐ Handful of raw ground beef or one uncooked hamburger patty
- ☐ Grill and utensils

Advance Prep

Hey, you're grilling out for this one. Easy, right? Besides reading the lesson and picking up the food, there isn't much to prep in advance. Don't forget to check the propane tank.

Running the Activity

You've grilled all the burgers (except one), everything is set to eat, and the kids are at the table. Perfect. Before serving the burgers, substitute a big mound of raw ground beef on one bun instead of the cooked patty. Or if you're using frozen patties, drop one of those hockey pucks on a bun.

Put the uncooked burger right on top of the serving platter of burgers, or you can put it on a separate plate and offer it to the kids first. Lift off the top of the bun so they get a good view of it. Point out that it hasn't been grilled, and see if anyone would like that one instead of a cooked one.

Teaching the Lesson

Raw (or frozen) burgers are not exactly appetizing. This burger needs to be cooked before it can be edible. Now, if this beef could talk, I'm not so sure it would like the idea of being placed on a grill over a searing fire. But without being cooked, this burger will never bring nourishment to anyone.

Sometimes we're a little like this raw burger. Before we can be of any good to others, God needs to make some changes in our lives. Sometimes we need to go through the fire, so to speak—and that isn't pleasant.

But if he doesn't do that, we'll never reach the potential he intends for us. We'll never bring "nourishment" to others like God wants us to.

- Can any of you think of an example of that?
- Can you think of a time when you had to go through something that wasn't fun but in the end helped make you a better person?

Let me share some Scripture verses with you.

Consider it pure joy, my brothers and sisters, whenever you face trials of many kinds, because you know that the testing of your faith produces perseverance. Let perseverance finish its work so that you may be mature and complete, not lacking anything. (James 1:2–4)

Sometimes God puts us "on the grill" as a way to test and strengthen our faith. It develops and deepens our Christian character so that we have perseverance . . .

the ability to hang in there and stay true to him in the tough times. It completes something in us. Makes us mature so that we don't come up short. In other words, the tough times help make us into the person we should be. The kind of person who lacks "nothing." Does that make sense?

- Let's hit one more aspect of this. Can you think of a time when you went through something that seemed like torture, but later you were able to help someone else because of that experience?

Check out this passage.

Praise be to the God and Father of our Lord Jesus Christ, the Father of compassion and the God of all comfort, who comforts us in all our troubles, so that we can comfort those in any trouble with the comfort we ourselves receive from God. (2 Cor. 1:3–4)

There are times God puts us on the grill not only for *our* good but also for the good of *others*. Once we've experienced certain trials and trouble we can relate to others like nobody else can. After we've gone through something hard, we're in a perfect place to help others who are going through a similar problem.

- Can you think of a time where you've helped someone get through a hard time because you'd gone through something similar?
- Do you think that's a good thing to remember when you're going through hard things?

Often, we go through trials to mature us. To protect us. To draw us close to good—for our own good. And sometimes we go through hard things so that we can truly help others.

Summing It Up

- Sometimes we go through tough times because of our own mistakes, our bad choices, or because of sin. This helps us to say no to sin the next time we're tempted.

- Other times we seem to go through tough times because God is protecting us, making us into better people, and maturing us for our own good.
- And still other times we go through some kind of suffering so that we'll be able to help others and be more understanding when they go through hard times.

For whatever reason we go through tough times, remember it's always for our own good—and for the good of others.

When you go through tough times, try to avoid complaining—and don't give up. A raw burger isn't at all appetizing. Only after it is fully cooked can it bring nourishment. Realize God cares enough about you to cook you a bit, to put you on the grill so that you'll be a better person, able to help others, and so that you'll be all-around more "appetizing" or appealing as a person, able to do the good work he's planned for you to do.

> So then, those who suffer according to God's will should commit themselves to their faithful Creator and continue to do good. (1 Pet. 4:19)

Having this perspective or understanding won't take away the pain of suffering, but it does make it a little easier to bear. And as that happens, guess what? You're already showing real signs of maturing. Flame on.

Catching Fire

THEME: Burning for God with passion versus being passive in our faith

KEEP IT SAFE

This lesson is designed to be done outdoors, away from anything flammable.

 ## THINGS YOU'LL NEED

- ☐ Tube of toothpaste
- ☐ Tube of diaper rash paste (I used Desitin brand, original formula)
- ☐ Tube of fire paste. You can pick this up online or at stores that have a decent camping department (the brand I used is Coghlan's). This stuff is amazing. It squeezes out like petroleum jelly, and when you put a

flame up to it, it catches fire and burns. It was designed to help start campfires and fires in fireplaces.

- ☐ Aluminum foil to wrap each tube of paste so the kids can't identify them
- ☐ Five-gallon bucket filled with water
- ☐ Three pieces of wood (I used 6 x 6 squares of scrap plywood, but other sizes of wood will work fine—as long as they'll easily fit in the bucket)
- ☐ Some kind of lighter. The lighter sticks used for starting a fire in a fireplace work fine. I've also used a small and inexpensive 14.1 ounce propane torch (like plumbers use) made by BernzOMatic, and I *loved* that. It also will be a little more intriguing for kids. You'll find BernzOMatic torches in the plumbing aisle at the hardware store.
- ☐ Ideally, some kind of fireproof gloves. They're often stocked at hardware stores, by the grilling gear. You could also use a simple oven mitt, but you lose the dexterity you'll get from fireproof gloves.

Advance Prep

I know, it looks like a lot of stuff to pick up. But this lesson is worth it. Totally. You'll be messing with fire, so do this one outside—a safe distance from anything flammable. And be sure to test the pastes out in advance to see how they burn. I've found I can clean off the wood squares and reuse them.

Cover the tubes with foil before the kids are around. Just leave the cap area exposed. You don't want the kids to see the labels on the tubes—especially the fire paste. All you need to do now is test this so you feel comfortable with it. Squirt a dab of each paste onto a piece of wood and apply the flame to see if it burns. Only the fire paste should truly ignite.

When you're done, dunk the pieces of wood in the five-gallon bucket of water—and let them soak there long enough to be sure you've extinguished any smoldering flame. Then clean off all the paste and leave the wood outside to dry. You're all set.

Running the Activity

Be sure the bucket is filled with water and is in close proximity. I keep it right by my feet. Have the kids make a three-inch X on each of the three pieces of wood, using a different paste each time. Keep the tube of paste by each wood sample so you can identify later which paste was used.

Tell the kids you want to light the paste, and you're looking to see which ignites and burns best.

Time to put on your fireproof gloves. Now, taking one piece of wood at a time, put the lighter or torch to it. Save the fire paste for last.

- The toothpaste won't do much—even with a torch.
- The diaper rash paste won't do much with a stick lighter, but with a torch you may find it sputters and sparks a little.
- The fire paste slowly ignites and burns until the entire X is aflame.

Submerge each of the pieces of wood in the bucket, then pull them out one at a time after you're sure the flames are completely extinguished. Now let the kids unwrap each tube of paste and set it with the corresponding piece of wood.

Teaching the Lesson

The three pastes represent different kinds of Christians—and how well they "burn" for Jesus. How intense they are for God.

- Some Christians never seem to ignite.
- Others sputter and spark but never really catch fire.
- Others catch fire and keep burning strong.

Let me read a familiar parable Jesus told. (Read Matthew 13:3–9, 18–23, the parable of the sower and the seed.)

- Jesus talked about how some people never seem to grow and mature as Christians. They are distracted. Lose their focus. Whatever. Was the problem with the seed or with the soil?

- When the toothpaste and the diaper rash paste wouldn't ignite, was the problem with the flame or with the paste?

The fire, like the seed in the parable, is a constant. The paste, like the soil in Jesus's example, was the thing that changed. Let's look at different kinds of Christians each paste might represent.

Toothpaste: some Christians are all about "looking good." They're all show and no go. They might have a nice Christian smile, but they really aren't burning for Christ inside. And likely they aren't truly living like a Christian should either.

Diaper rash paste: some Christians seem to have stops and starts. They burn for short bursts, but then the fire goes out. They can't seem to stay ignited for Jesus on their own. They aren't mature. Steady. They need help. They need to be fed—and don't really feed themselves.

Fire paste: this represents Christians who burn steadily. Consistently. Even when nobody is there prompting them to.

- What kind of Christian do you want to be?
- How do you think you'll get there?

Let's look at some starting points for being the type of Christian who burns with a steady dedication for God.

- **Burning hot for God is a heart issue.** Look at King David's psalms. He burned hot for God because he truly had a heart for God. Encourage your kids to think about that. If they want to burn for God, one thing they can do is ask God to help give them a heart for him.

- **Remember what God has done for us.** It seems to me that those who never forget how God rescued them tend to burn hotter for him.

- **It's a choice.** Time after time we must choose God and obedience to him. When we ignore the prompting of the Holy Spirit and when we know the right thing to do—but don't do it—we are "quenching" the impact of the Holy Spirit in our lives. When we quench the Spirit . . . we quench our own fire.

Summing It Up

Three different pastes, but only one burned consistently. I have no idea what the percentages are, but I'm not sure even one in three "Christians" truly burns hot and steady for God. Which means many of your friends will not. They'll make choices consistent with passive Christians, not passionate ones. If you choose to be a Christian who burns hot for God, I believe you'll never regret that.

- It's my prayer that you'll have a heart that burns strong and steady for God. That you are passionate for God, not passive.
- It's my prayer that you'll ask God to give you a heart that desires him enough to say no to compromise.
- I pray you'll choose to obey God and his Word from your heart, not because you have to.
- I pray you'll never forget that he's chosen you . . . he's chosen to rescue you. And for that, we should be forever grateful and dedicated to him. May you always burn for him.

Surf's Up

THEME: Real friends—how to be one / what to look for in one

THINGS YOU'LL NEED

☐ At least eight balloons—the big, full-sized ones. (Use four when you take a practice run on this and four with the kids.) You can find durable, bigger balloons at a party store. They often sell them in small bags according to color. Wherever you buy the balloons, just be sure they're big—and not the ultra-thin cheap things. Avoid the water-balloon size.

☐ A piece of plywood roughly 2 x 3 feet—and at least a half-inch thick. When I did this lesson, I actually used a giant baking pan from the church kitchen. It was 24 x 30 inches with a small lip on it. The pan was commercial strength and worked perfectly.

Advance Prep

You'll need to test this out. Blow up four balloons so they're nice and big, and pretty equal in size. Lay the plywood on the floor, then lift one end at a time and slip the four balloons underneath—one below each corner. Is the plywood balancing on the four balloons? Okay, perfect.

Now, the trick is to stand on the platform without the balloons breaking. Totally possible. I've done this successfully with some really big high school students. Stepping up onto the platform generally requires one or two people to help you balance. Without that help, you'll likely fall.

Once you're on board and steady, your helper(s) can let go. Now get in a surfer stance and try to wiggle around a bit. Congratulations . . . you're surfing.

Running the Activity

Have the kids help you put the plywood on the four inflated balloons. Then let each one take a turn to try standing on top. They'll need to work together, just like you needed help, to steady each other while each has a chance to get on top of the board and find their balance.

Encourage each one to show off their best surfing moves. You might even grab a video clip. Be sure one or two others are close by and working as spotters (could be brothers, sisters, spouse, you) to steady them when they lose their balance. This is important, because doing so will set things up to convey the spiritual nugget of truth afterward.

Teaching the Lesson

Balancing on the balloons was tricky—but it became entirely possible when we had a little help from others.

This is a picture of life. Sometimes it's easy to lose our perspective or to get off balance somehow if we don't have someone coming alongside to round out our viewpoint. Having a good friend or family member close can really help keep you from falling or getting hurt in so many ways. Here are some things good friends or siblings can do for you.

- They can help you stay "balanced" when you're in a precarious situation.
- They can help give you perspective when you may be off the bubble—when your viewpoint about something or someone isn't quite balanced.
- They can help give you strength and encouragement to keep going.
- They can help you succeed where you may have failed alone.
- They can help keep you from falling into sin and temptation.
- They can warn you of danger or if they think you're making a mistake.
- They can urge you on to mature as a Christian and to obey God's Word.
- They can bring laughter and fun into your life.
- They can chase away the shadows of loneliness, doubt, and fear.

We could go on, but having a good friend is pretty important in life. One of the famous friendships in the Bible was between David and Jonathan. Over and over these friends were there for each other.

Jonathan warned David of danger in 1 Samuel 20 and helped him escape. When David was on the run, being hunted by King Saul and his army, Jonathan risked his life to see his friend. He encouraged David and helped him find strength in the Lord.

> While David was at Horesh in the desert of Ziph, he learned that Saul had come out to take his life. And Saul's son Jonathan went to David at Horesh and helped him find strength in God. "Don't be afraid," he said. "My father Saul will not lay a hand on you. You will be king over Israel, and I will be second to you. Even my father Saul knows this." The two of them made a covenant before the Lord. Then Jonathan went home, but David remained at Horesh. (1 Sam. 23:15–18)

That's what true friends do.

- They encourage.
- They protect.
- They stand by you.
- And ultimately they strengthen you in the Lord if they're a Christian.

That's the type of friend I hope you are to your brothers, sisters, and others. Is that the type of friend you want to be?

And if that is the type of friend you want to be, is there anything you know you need to change, correct, fix, or apologize for to your friend? Or is there a way you want to work harder at being a good friend?

I hope you each grow to have at least one friend like that . . . one who will be a Jonathan to you.

If you want good friends, you need to *be* a good friend. Take a look at the list I read earlier—that list of things a good friend can and should be.

If the friends you have aren't the type who strengthen you in the Lord, or encourage you in your faith, you need to think about that. Maybe you need to develop a new friendship or two.

If you want a friend who will help strengthen you in the Lord, be sure that friend is committed to God too. Make sure they have good character and morals and also have some good sense and wisdom. Here are a few verses that may help you.

> Walk with the wise and become wise,
>   for a companion of fools suffers harm. (Prov. 13:20)

Do not be misled. "Bad company corrupts good character." (1 Cor. 15:33)

> Do not make friends with a hot-tempered person,
>   do not associate with one easily angered,
> or you may learn their ways
>   and get yourself ensnared. (Prov. 22:24–25)

Ask God to lead you to the person who can be a good friend. Remember, the person God wants you to befriend may not be the one you would expect, so keep your eyes open. That person probably isn't surrounded by a bunch of friends already. Likely they want a true friend as badly as you do.

A Special Word for Parents

Be sensitive. Keep your eyes open. Your kids need good friends. They may need help building good friendships. If your son or daughter struggles to find good friends, or you're not sure of the type of friends they're making, let me mention a couple of quick things to you.

- Make your home a hangout. Stock the fridge and the freezer and encourage your kids to have their friends over. What better way to see the types of friends they're making?

- Be sure you're getting your kids to church every week. Having a solid Christian as your closest friend is wise. There is likely a higher concentration of Christian kids at church. I've worked with students on a volunteer basis for over twenty-five years, and I've seen this over and over. If you don't make the effort to get your kids to church and out to the youth group every week, they won't feel as connected. So where are they going to make their closest friends?

- And think about how involved in sports you want your kids to be. Sports can be great, but if it means that practice and games are keeping your kids from being at church consistently, you may be making a strategic error. If the kids don't attend church weekly, their closest friendships will likely develop at school. If their school friends are solid Christians, great. If not, think where those friendships will lead. Those friends will have a bigger influence on your kids in their teenage years than you will.

- I wanted my kids to develop those close friendships at church, with solid Christian kids. So we limited sports involvement, and even when they were in sports, we made sure they didn't miss a church youth group event—even if it meant getting them to church late. Did it mean some extra driving? Of course. Was it inconvenient? Totally. But would my wife and I do it the same way again if we had the chance? Absolutely.

- One last thing I've observed with the youth group. Sometimes parents are tired, busy, or self-absorbed when it comes time to pick kids up after youth events at church. They are in a big fat rush to get their kids out of the church and into the car. Mistake. Get your kids to the youth group event early if you can. Let them stay late. Those are huge social strengthening times. Give them an extra fifteen minutes. Offer to give their friends a ride home. Whip through a drive-thru and pick up a treat on the way home. You'll be making a wise investment.

Summing It Up

Good friends are important. They can help you, keep you balanced, and keep you from falling. Make sure you build good Christian friendships and be the kind of friend to others that you want them to be to you.

One more thing. We have Jesus . . . and he can be our truest friend. Read John 15:9–17.

Snow Fort

THEME: **Doing things that count for eternity**

THINGS YOU'LL NEED

- ☐ Good snow
- ☐ Snow shovels (a coal shovel-type works great if you're working on a plowed pile)
- ☐ Light sticks (from the dollar store) if you're doing this at night
- ☐ Hot cocoa (optional) to enjoy while you tie in the devotional

Advance Prep

Watch the weather report or simply wait for a good snow. When the conditions are right, you're ready to go. When I shovel my driveway, I tend to shovel the snow into one big pile so I have something to work with rather than just tossing it to either side.

Running the Activity

Get the kids outside to build a snow fort. If you've had snow in the area but can't scrape together enough snow at your place to make a fort, get in the car and find a spot. Is there a parking lot at church where they've plowed snow into a pile? That will work.

Have fun carving out a fort, hopefully with a small tunnel. Always supervise the kids—tunnels can collapse. If you're doing this at night, crack open the light sticks and poke them into the tunnel ceiling for a creepy glow.

Work on the fort long enough to make something good but not so long that the kids are tired of it or are getting too cold. Take some pictures of the fort to refer to later. Break out the hot cocoa right there or go back in the house. While they're sipping on the cocoa, tie this together.

Teaching the Lesson

- Making a snow fort is fun, but what's going to happen to it when we get a couple of days in a row with a temperature above freezing?
- Snow forts won't last. How are they like some other things we do or spend time on in life?
- In life, sometimes we spend a lot of time and effort on things that won't last or matter. We spend time doing or watching things that won't count for eternity. Can you give me any examples?

Now, I'm not saying we can't go out and enjoy ourselves or others. But sometimes we need to think about what we're doing. If all we're ever doing is building "snow forts," spending time on things that will melt away and not matter for eternity, we need to rethink things a little. Does that make sense?

God gives us time, resources (abilities and opportunities), and the total freedom to choose how we spend them. Too often we spend our time, our abilities, and our freedom on things that won't last. They won't matter for eternity. That doesn't sound smart to me.

Jesus warned us to be careful where we invest ourselves.

Do not store up for yourselves treasures on earth, where moths and vermin destroy, and where thieves break in and steal. But store up for yourselves treasures in heaven, where moths and vermin do not destroy, and where thieves do not break in and steal. For where your treasure is, there your heart will be also. (Matt. 6:19–21)

- How do we store up treasures in heaven?
- Do you think that every time you resist temptation, you're storing up treasure in heaven?
- Do you think that every time you tell someone about Jesus, you're storing up treasure in heaven?
- Do you think that every time you are kind to someone, even if they aren't your friend, you're storing up treasure in heaven?
- Do you think that every time you honor and obey Mom or Dad, you're storing up treasure in heaven?
- Do you think that every time you read your Bible or pray, you're storing up treasure in heaven?
- Why is it so important that our hearts be focused more on eternity than on this world?

Remember, God put us here on earth, and he saved us for a purpose. He designed us to do some things.

For we are God's handiwork, created in Christ Jesus to do good works, which God prepared in advance for us to do. (Eph. 2:10)

Summing It Up

There's one more verse I'd like to read to you.

You who are young, be happy while you are young, and let your heart give you joy in the days of your youth. Follow the ways of your heart and whatever your eyes see, but know that for all these things God will bring you into judgment. (Eccles. 11:9)

You're young. You want to enjoy life. You want to have fun. I get that. So does God. But he reminds us in his Word that he put us here for specific reasons—and that we'll be judged on how we use this life and the abilities and opportunities he gives us. Let's make sure we're not spending all our time and energy on things that will melt away like that snow fort. Let's be looking to do things that will last for eternity.

Christianity and the $2 Bill

THEME: A true relationship with Christ changes everything and should make us inseparable from Christ

THINGS YOU'LL NEED

☐ A $2 bill for yourself and *each* of the kids to keep (available at banks)
☐ At least two $1 bills

Advance Prep

Start checking at banks early to pick up enough $2 bills. They can be hard to find at times, so don't expect to stop at the bank to get them on the way home the day you plan to do this lesson. You may have to stop at a handful of banks.

This is one of those rare sessions when practicing something in advance isn't necessary. Maybe you'll want to put some extra time in thought and prayer about *your* relationship with Christ instead. Are there some areas you need to work on? It will be hard to teach the kids if you aren't practicing the principles yourself.

Running the Activity

This lesson is low on activity, so I'd definitely plan to take the family to a fast-food restaurant, pick up snacks for each of the kids, and do this one right there around a table. The food will help keep them occupied—and listening. While the kids are eating, place the two singles down on the table. Then lay a $2 bill next to them.

- Imagine I'm going to give each of you two dollars. What would you choose, two singles or a $2 bill?
- There's something about a $2 bill that gives it extra value—even though the two singles are worth the same amount of money. Maybe it's because the $2 bill is more unique or rare. You don't see one every day.
- The $2 bill reminds me of something else you don't see often. Christians who are following Christ—clinging tightly to him—all week long.

Teaching the Lesson

Take a look at a $1 bill. Let's imagine it represents our lives before we became a Christian.

- **In many ways, we were our own person**—or at least we liked to think of ourselves that way.
- **In many ways, we spent ourselves however we chose to.** We decided how to use our time, our abilities, and the resources and opportunities we had.

But in reality—before we were a Christian—we were still answering to someone—and I'm not talking about parents here.

- **The Bible says we were all slaves to sin.** Sin was our master.

When we became a follower of Christ, we were freed from our old master and forever joined with Jesus Christ.

But thanks be to God that, though you used to be slaves to sin, you have come to obey from your heart the pattern of teaching that has now claimed your allegiance. You have been set free from sin and have become slaves to righteousness. (Rom. 6:17–18)

Now look at the front of this $2 bill. This represents our being forever joined together with Christ.

- If we are a slave to Christ, can we "spend" ourselves any way we want to?
- If we are forever joined with Christ, can we live one way at school or church—and another way with friends or family?

No . . . we are forever joined with Christ.

- He is always with us—even when nobody else is.
- He knows our every thought—and knows everything we do and say.

If we are joined with Christ, we're expected to live in a way that gives a positive reflection of Christ—not a negative one. We can't go back to living however we want to live.

Just as you used to offer yourselves as slaves to impurity and to ever-increasing wickedness, so now offer yourselves as slaves to righteousness leading to holiness. When you were slaves to sin, you were free from the control of righteousness. What benefit did you reap at that time from the things you are now ashamed of? Those things result in death! But now that you have been set free from sin and have become slaves of God, the benefit you reap leads to holiness, and the result is eternal life. (vv. 19–22)

Flip the $2 bill over to view the back side. This is an artist's rendition of the signing of the Declaration of Independence. In essence, the signers of the Declaration of Independence basically said that they were no longer going to serve Britain. They were going to serve a new master from now on.

- This was a dangerous and brave thing these men did. When they signed the Declaration of Independence, it was an act of war—and a no-turning-back decision.

- If they failed, they would be guilty of treason, which was punishable by death.
- Once they made the decision to sign the Declaration of Independence, it meant that everything changed. They couldn't live as followers of the king of England at some times and then as true-blue independent colonists at other times.
- They gave up the temporary comforts of serving Britain. They were looking ahead—at what would be good for them in the long run.

It's similar for us as Christians.

- In our world, it can be dangerous to switch masters—to name Jesus Christ as our Lord.
- Making a decision to follow Christ is a no-turning-back decision that impacts every part of our lives.
- We can't serve sin sometimes, then serve Jesus at other times. We are joined with him. Together. Inseparable.
- Following Christ is turning our backs on some of the comforts and thrills of serving sin. It is looking ahead—and living now with eternity in mind.

Can we go back to living like a $1 bill again? Sure, but why would we want to? The Bible warns of the dangers of going back and living like sin was our master again. If we allow sin a toehold in our lives, it can gain a stronghold.

Don't you know that when you offer yourselves to someone as obedient slaves, you are slaves of the one you obey—whether you are slaves to sin, which leads to death, or to obedience, which leads to righteousness? (v. 16)

Summing It Up

Therefore, if anyone is in Christ, the new creation has come: The old has gone, the new is here! (2 Cor. 5:17)

- As Christians, we are a new creation, the Bible tells us.
- We're not a single dollar anymore. We can't spend ourselves any way we want.

- We are forever joined with Christ.
- We need to live as a follower of Christ should.

Don't let anyone look down on you because you are young, but set an example for the believers in speech, in conduct, in love, in faith and in purity. (1 Tim. 4:12)

I'd like each of you to keep a $2 bill. Don't spend it but rather let it be a reminder that you are joined with Christ.

- We are a new creation.
- We are to live different from the world.
- We have a new master—and we no longer want to serve the old one.
- Living like this is rare but has great value.

Brain Dead

THEME: Guarding our minds against anything other than a truly Christian worldview

THINGS YOU'LL NEED

- [ ] A Jell-O mold, which can be round to represent a brain—or better yet, pick up one that's actually *shaped* like a brain. I got mine at American Science and Surplus (www.sciplus.com). I've also seen them at Educational Innovations (www.teachersource.com). I've seen them marketed online as "zombie brain molds" as well.
- [ ] Jell-O, enough boxes to fit the mold you choose. Ideally, make one entire Jell-O mold for each of the kids who will be present.
- [ ] Ladder—or a second-story window to drop the Jell-O from

Advance Prep

This lesson doesn't require you to actually practice it, but you'll need to have the Jell-O made in advance.

If you're able to pick up a brain-shaped Jell-O mold, that extra effort will pay off with an extra wow-factor as you start. And if it helps with the decision, consider these two thoughts.

- Every time you use the mold just for fun, in the future, it will serve as a reminder of this lesson.
- Later in this book, we'll teach a different lesson using the same Jell-O mold. If you want a sneak peek at that one, look for lesson 24, "Brain Food." The point is if you get the brain mold, you'll use it again.

It will require a little more prep time, but making one complete Jell-O brain for each of the kids will help you make the strongest impression—and the kids will definitely have more fun.

Have the Jell-O completely made, out of the mold, on a plate, and ready to go before the kids get involved. If you're making multiple brains, pick up different colored Jell-O mixes for each.

The idea is that you're going to drop the gelatin brains from a height so that they splatter upon impact. So decide if you'll drop them from a ladder or a second-story window. If the kids are going to help you drop them, keep the safety factor in mind when choosing your launch pad.

Running the Activity

Get the kids together and present each of them with a Jell-O brain. Explain that you're going to drop the brains and watch them splatter. At this moment, you have their complete attention. This is important, because it means that they'll remember the lesson just that much better.

Have each one carry their brain to the designated drop spot. If you feel comfortable letting them drop it from the ladder or second story, great. If not, take the Jell-O brains one at a time, and you can do the honors.

Once they've splattered, don't bother cleaning up the mess yet. First, you're going to want to tie in the lesson before their attention drifts.

Teaching the Lesson

A Jell-O brain is a really fragile thing. It doesn't take much to damage or destroy it, right?

In real life, the brains in our heads are very similar. They are fragile. That's one reason God encased our brains in bone. Our skulls work like built-in helmets.

Sometimes people wear extra protection for the sole purpose of protecting their brains while they're doing something active or playing sports. Can you name some sports, activities, or occupations in life when people wear some kind of helmet or other protective headgear?

Protecting the brain *physically* is important. And we need to protect our brains *spiritually* as well. We need to guard how we think—especially so we don't buy into the enemy's lies.

We live in a world that is constantly trying to move away from what God says is true and right—and shift our beliefs and thinking as well. Through movies, games, music, the internet, celebrities, persuasive people, friends, books, and textbooks, the views and opinions of this world are getting inside our skulls. Many of these views are not at all in agreement with the Bible. Unless we actively work to combat this, the views of this world will mess with our brains and change how we see life, the world we live in, the Bible, and God himself.

As Christians, we need to guard our minds. What are some of the ways the world is trying to change our thinking—often in ways that are contrary to clear commands in the Bible? (*Note*: share only the things that you think are age appropriate.)

- The world wants us to think that the Word of God is full of errors and isn't completely true.
- The world wants us to believe that some of the principles, commands, and so on in God's Word don't apply anymore.
- Our world says people are basically good. The Bible says people are evil and need salvation.

- Our world says there is no absolute truth, no absolute standard for right living. The Bible says there is a way that we're to live and outlines it for us.

- Our world says sex before marriage is perfectly acceptable and good. The Bible says the opposite.

- Our world has redefined sex, as in what is considered sex and what is not considered sex. Like "Oral sex is not really having sex," or "Pornography is okay." The Bible clearly speaks against sex outside marriage.

- Even the church gets sucked into believing things that are twists of Scripture. For example, some churches preach that God wants us to be healthy and wealthy, and if we have enough faith, God will bless us with health and wealth. The Bible gives a very different picture. Our true rewards come when we get to heaven, not while we're here on earth.

- Our world, and even many churches, say homosexuality should be embraced. God is a God of love, right? Actually, God has clear boundaries on acceptable sexual relations. Sex before marriage is wrong. If you're married, sex with someone other than your mate is wrong. Sex with the same sex is wrong. We can have all kinds of sex drives, but God commands that we follow his ways, even if we have natural desires outside of what he allows. He calls us to self-control. God doesn't change, and neither does his Word. Yes, God is a God of love—but also a God of justice. We must do what is right.

We could go on and on with other issues that the world sees differently than God does in his Word.

What if I raised you to believe that you could fly—as in flap your arms like wings? What if that same message was reinforced in movies you watched, music you listened to, and by others in your life? What if it was taught to you in your school textbooks? If you truly believed you could fly, would you be able to?

If I took you to the edge of the Grand Canyon and told you to jump off the cliff and fly, you'd end up looking like that Jell-O brain, no matter how hard you flapped your arms, right?

In a similar way, if what we believe in life—and the actions we take—are not based on God's truth, we're heading for trouble.

How do we make sure we're not drawn away into believing the lies this world wants us to believe? How do we protect the fragile minds we have?

- We need to stay in God's Word and believe that the Bible is our source of truth in a world of lies.
- We need to go to a church where the Word of God is carefully and accurately preached.
- We need to obey what God says in his Word and consistently put it into practice.

By filling our minds with God's truth—and obeying God's Word—we'll be protecting our minds from believing and being hurt by the world's lies.

Summing It Up

The Bible is our source of truth. The enemy wants to twist it so we don't obey the truth of the Word . . . so we get hurt or become ineffective Christians as a result. Wrong teaching can even come from the church or high-profile Christians.

> Even from your own number men will arise and distort the truth in order to draw away disciples after them. So be on your guard! (Acts 20:30–31)

If we're not reading the Bible, won't it be easy for us to get deceived by the enemy?

We need to read this Bible God has given us. We need to ask him to help us interpret it correctly.

> Do your best to present yourself to God as one approved, a worker who does not need to be ashamed and who correctly handles the word of truth. (2 Tim. 2:15)

And we need to actually do what the Bible teaches us to do. By doing these things we'll guard our minds. We'll know the truth—and we'll be able to combat the lies of the enemy and this world.

Our brains are fragile, like Jell-O. They need to be protected. We need to guard our minds. We need to keep from being deceived into wrong perspectives and thinking that will cause us to make mistakes. We do this by filtering everything going on around us through the truth of the Bible, God's Word. Does that make sense?

> Blessed is the one
>> who does not walk in step with the wicked
> or stand in the way that sinners take
>> or sit in the company of mockers,
> but whose delight is in the law of the Lord,
>> and who meditates on his law day and night.
> That person is like a tree planted by streams of water,
>> which yields its fruit in season
> and whose leaf does not wither—
>> whatever they do prospers.
>
> Not so the wicked!
>> They are like chaff
>> that the wind blows away.
> Therefore the wicked will not stand in the judgment,
>> nor sinners in the assembly of the righteous.
>
> For the Lord watches over the way of the righteous,
>> but the way of the wicked leads to destruction. (Ps. 1)

Life Lessons
from a Graveyard

THEME: Importance/value of building and guarding a genuinely good reputation

THINGS YOU'LL NEED

- ☐ A local cemetery to visit
- ☐ Paper and pen for each of the kids
- ☐ A library book that lists some epitaphs or a printout of some interesting epitaphs you find with an online search

Advance Prep

Personally visit the cemetery in advance. You want to be sure you'll be bringing the kids to a cemetery that has some key features.

- **Headstones with epitaphs.** Those one- or two-line commentaries on the deceased person's life are what we're really looking for. They're rare these days, so an older cemetery is preferable.
- **Exotic grave markers.** Often seen in the older cemeteries, these statues and monuments will hold the group's attention more than a cemetery with grave markers flush to the ground.
- **Interesting or historic people.** Check online or call the cemetery office and ask if there are any "persons of interest," and check them out so you'll know where to take the kids when you come back.

One last note for prep. If you pick up a library book of epitaphs, thumb through it a bit and note some interesting or unusual epitaphs you'll want to share with the kids. You might even find some celebrity epitaphs if you check online.

Running the Activity

To make things more interesting, don't tell the kids where you plan to take them. You might tell them something cryptic like, "I'm taking you someplace where each of you will go on your own—eventually—whether or not you want to." Yeah, I know. That's kind of creepy. But you do want to get them thinking here.

When you get to the cemetery, give each of them paper and a pen (unless they have a smartphone) and explain what you'd like them to do.

- Ask them to look for epitaphs and write some down (or snap a photo of them).
- Ask them to notice or take a picture of interesting or unusual tombstones and monuments as they wander through the designated area. It may be the spookiest ones they see, the most unusual names, the strangest monument, and so on.
- Remind them to be respectful of the grounds and the people buried there, especially if mourners are present.

Give them set boundaries—a designated area. Also give them a set period of time. Ten to fifteen minutes should do. They can work together or individually, your call. You may want to do the above yourself too so you have that much more material to share with the kids.

Teaching the Lesson

After the time is up, have the kids share some of their findings, especially the epitaphs.

Share any epitaphs you wrote down from the cemetery or ones you gathered in advance. Read some funny, sad, or absurd ones. Did you get any examples from the headstones of celebrities or famous people? Now is the time to share these as you move into the spiritual truth of the lesson.

Basically, an epitaph is a tombstone inscription giving you a bit of information about the deceased person. Maybe it sums up their life in a line or two or tells how that person was loved or something the person will be remembered for.

Did you know that God wrote epitaphs of sorts for people in the Bible? They may not have been etched on a tombstone, but he recorded them for all time in the pages of Scripture.

I'm going to read some examples of how God summed up a person's life, whether good or bad. See if you can guess who each one is written about.

1. "He disappeared, because God took him. For before he was taken up, he was known as a person who pleased God."
   Enoch; see Hebrews 11:5 and Genesis 5:24

2. "He obeyed God, who warned him about things that had never happened before. By his faith he condemned the rest of the world, and he received the righteousness that comes by faith."
   Noah; Hebrews 11:7

3. "He chose to share the oppression of God's people instead of enjoying the fleeting pleasures of sin. He thought it was better to suffer for the sake of Christ than to own the treasures of Egypt, for he was looking ahead to his great reward."
   Moses; Hebrews 11:25–26

4. "But he did what was evil in the LORD's sight."

   King Jehoahaz; 2 Kings 13:2 (The same was true of many other Old Testament kings.)

5. "He did much that was evil in the LORD's sight, arousing his anger."

   King Manasseh; 2 Kings 21:6

6. "In this way, _____ did what was evil in the LORD's sight; he refused to follow the LORD completely, as his father, David, had done."

   King Solomon; 1 Kings 11:6

Someday each of us will be buried under some kind of tombstone, unless Jesus comes first.

If you died today, what might your epitaph say?

- "His sister was a real jerk, and he made sure she knew it."
- "She always wanted to be a good kid. Too bad she rarely got around to it."
- "His parents thought he was the perfect son. His friends knew better."
- "He thought he could get away with it."

An epitaph records something a person is remembered for. It's about a person's reputation. If you died today, what would you *like* your epitaph to say?

- Can you think of someone you really look up to, living or dead—someone with a good reputation?
- Would one of you like to share about that person?
- How valuable is a good name or a good reputation? Why?

Here are some things the Bible says about somebody's name or reputation.

> We have happy memories of the godly,
>> but the name of a wicked person rots away. (Prov. 10:7 NLT)

> Choose a good reputation over great riches;
>> being held in high esteem is better than silver or gold. (22:1 NLT)

If a good reputation is that valuable, we ought to go after it. How do we build a good reputation? Listen to what the Word says about that.

> Never let *loyalty* and *kindness* leave you!
> Tie them around your neck as a reminder.
> Write them deep within your heart.
> Then you will find favor with both God and people,
> and you will earn a good reputation. (3:3–4 NLT, emphasis added)

If we are loyal and kind, we'll be building a good reputation.

A good reputation is something we *earn*. It is something we *build consistently* over time. Listen to 1 Timothy 4:12. This verse really sums up what it is to have a good reputation.

> Don't let anyone think less of you because you are young. Be an example to all believers in what you say, in the way you live, in your love, your faith, and your purity. (NLT)

What kind of reputation are we building in the areas the verse mentions?

- The things we say.
- The way we live.
- The way we treat and love others.
- The faith we have in God and our obedience to his principles.
- The area of purity.

It takes a long time to build a good reputation. How long does it take to damage or destroy one? Can any of you share a real-life example?

Summing It Up

If we had a pile of gold, we'd protect it, right? If a good reputation is more valuable than gold, as we read in Proverbs 22:1, we'd better protect our reputation even *more*. How can we protect our reputation?

There are plenty of headstones that simply record a name, a date of birth, and a date of death. No details of their life are given. All we know is that they existed.

I want more than that for my life. And I hope you want more for your life too.

I'm going to read Hebrews 11:32–39. This is like a whole bunch of epitaphs rolled up in a few verses. It talks about people who finished well. Many of them faced death because they would not compromise and ruin their reputation as a Christian. (Read those verses aloud now.)

I'm going to reread the start of verse 39; it sums all this up. "All these people earned a good reputation because of their faith."

It all comes down to how we live out our faith, doesn't it? I don't want to have a bad reputation, a bad name in the sight of God or other people. I don't want to just exist either. I want to build a good reputation, a good name. Want to join me?

Sick Smoothie

THEME: Living right for God in gratitude for his love

THINGS YOU'LL NEED

- ☐ Blender or smoothie maker. Don't have one? Improvise. Make an ice-cream sundae or a shake and add some nasty ingredient. The devotional will still work perfectly.
- ☐ Cup for each of the kids
- ☐ Ingredients for the smoothie (or other concoction): ice, fruit, and so on. If you need ideas, do a quick search online for "smoothie recipes." You'll find plenty.
- ☐ Nasty ingredient(s). This can be whatever you'd like. It can be something gross but still edible, like mayonnaise or horseradish. You'll want to add quite a bit of it to your smoothie to make sure the kids definitely don't want to taste it. Some of you may choose to use an ingredient far less appetizing—even sick—like the little presents pets leave you after they've eaten a big meal. If you choose something like that, you can be sure the kids will get the point of this lesson very clearly, but

remember you're going to have to sterilize the blender afterward. That's not the kind of thing you want to forget!

Advance Prep

Unless you're a smoothie master, get your ingredients together and practice making a smoothie so you're a little, well, smoother when you're doing it with the kids.

Don't add the Mr. Nasty ingredient(s) this time. You'll add that only when you do the devotional with the kids.

Now, one more big thing on the prep end. *Big.* Be sure to read this devotional all the way through beforehand. There is something toward the end of the "Summing It Up" section that you really need to consider ahead of time.

Running the Activity

Make smoothies with the kids. It's your call how much you involve them, but they'll be more into the devotional if they can help.

Make a delicious smoothie to begin with and pour a small amount in a cup for each to sample. Give them only a taste . . . you want them hungry for more.

Now bring out the Mr. Nasty ingredient(s) and add generous amounts to your already perfect smoothie. Make sure the kids know exactly what gross things you're adding. *You want them to feel that you're ruining a perfectly good smoothie.* Blend it up anyway, and then offer to fill their cups. If they protest or decline your offer, you've set things up perfectly to move on. Nice job.

Teaching the Lesson

A smoothie is supposed to be good and refreshing. The nasty ingredient(s) changed everything. Before I added the nasty ingredient(s), all of you were ready for a refill. Now none of you are anxious for the smoothie at all.

- Is this the kind of smoothie you'd expect me to offer to a guest in our house?
- Is this the kind of smoothie you'd expect me to offer to someone I love?
- Is this the kind of smoothie you'd expect me to give as an act of gratitude to someone who did something truly wonderful for me?

This sick smoothie parallels life in some ways. Imagine *we're* a smoothie. According to Romans 12:1, as an act of gratitude to God for his mercy on us, for his great love, for the way he saved us . . . we're to offer our lives as a sacrifice to him. As a gift. Sometimes we forget that and allow some things in our lives that are sick. Nasty. Things that don't belong in a Christian's life at all. And we offer this life to God.

What kinds of things do we allow to be part of our lives that shouldn't be there at all? Hypocrisy. Jealousy. Pride. Selfishness. Laziness. Complacency. Dishonesty. Disrespect. Disobedience. Anger. Unkindness to others. Anything you'd add?

Summing It Up

Let's look at Romans 12:1.

> And so, dear brothers and sisters, I plead with you to give your bodies to God because of all he has done for you. Let them be a living and holy sacrifice—the kind he will find acceptable. This is truly the way to worship him. (NLT)

Let me put that verse very loosely in my own words—with the whole smoothie thing in mind.

I beg you to hear me on this . . . because this is important. Our lives are to be like a gift we offer to God in gratitude for all he's done for us. It only makes sense that we work to be sure that this life we offer him is pleasing to him—without adding a bunch of nasty stuff. Which means we're going to be holy, or set apart for him. That means we're going to strive to obey him and his Word. As a way of showing our appreciation for what he's done for us, I urge you to worship God in this way.

Can you think of any things or attitudes in your life that really don't belong there—like the nasty stuff we added to the smoothie?

- What would you like to see change? What would you like to eliminate from your life so that you're appetizing and pleasing to God . . . so that you're like a great-tasting smoothie for him? How can I help you do that?

A Special Word for Parents

Now, I'm thinking this could be a really exceptional devotional if you let yourself be vulnerable. Ask your kids if there is anything they see in your life that they don't think really belongs there.

Whoa.

Not a comfortable question to ask the kids, right? Especially if you have teenagers. But ask it. And ask your spouse too—privately.

And be really, really careful how you respond to the kids or your spouse. You've got one shot at this. If you get all defensive or annoyed, don't expect them to give you input again. They'll still wish you were different, but they just won't tell you about it. That's not what you want.

If your spouse or kids share *anything* they wish you would change, anything they don't feel belongs in your life as a Christian, then, by God's grace, resolve to work on it. Muscle up a little self-control and ask the Holy Spirit for help. Make the changes. Do you have any idea how big this can be? This is leading by example, my friend. This will stick with them. They'll remember it—and their respect for you will grow.

Marshmallow Man

THEME: The devastating effects of pride

THINGS YOU'LL NEED

- ☐ Marshmallows, two different sizes. You can use the miniature ones for arms and legs and the bigger ones for the head and body, or the bigger ones for the arms and legs and the giant s'more-type marshmallows for the head and body. Pick up enough marshmallows so that each of the kids can make their own marshmallow man.
- ☐ Wooden toothpicks (get a box of them)
- ☐ Paper plates (one for each kid)
- ☐ Permanent marker
- ☐ Microwave oven
- ☐ Oven mitt
- ☐ Bucket of water

Advance Prep

Make your own marshmallow man in advance using the wooden toothpicks to hold together the body, arms, and legs. Skewer the marshmallows on the toothpicks like a shish kebab. I use four miniature marshmallows for each arm and leg and three regular marshmallows stacked for the head and body.

If I'm using the giant marshmallows, I generally use two regular marshmallows for each arm and leg and three giant ones for the head and body. When using giant marshmallows, you'll likely need extra toothpicks to hold everything together.

Use the marker to make eyes, nose, and a mouth. Put your marshmallow man on a paper plate and slide it in the microwave with the timer set for a minute or two. No more than that. You need to know how fast the marshmallow man expands—and it doesn't take long. Remember, the marshmallows will be superhot—like molten lava inside—so use your head. Use oven mitts too, if you pull the plate out of the microwave.

If you're using the miniature/regular marshmallow combination, you'll likely notice that the chest area of the marshmallow man starts to turn brown after it has hit its maximum expansion. Realize that if you leave it in the microwave much longer, the marshmallows will ignite.

When I get a flame, I stop the microwave immediately, open the door, and blow it out. Kids love seeing the flame, but you don't have to let it go that far. If you're going to take it to the point of flames, have a bucket of water handy so you can drop the plate in if needed as an extra safety precaution.

If you use the regular/giant marshmallow combination, realize that the marshmallow man will expand to a much larger size, which is also fun. Likely it will get so big that you'll have to stop the microwave before it browns, or else the marshmallows will start hitting the insides of the microwave, making a sticky mess.

You'll notice that after the marshmallow man cools, it shrinks, deflates, and hardens somewhat.

Running the Activity

Have each of the kids make a marshmallow man on a separate paper plate. Put their name on the plate with a marker. If you have a lot of kids, you may want to cook one or two marshmallow men in the microwave, then talk about what happened before microwaving the others. That may make it easier to hold their attention while you talk.

Let the kids watch in the microwave window as the marshmallow man cooks and expands into a monstrous mutant marshmallow man. When it has grown as big as you want to make it, take the plate out and give it a little shake. The steaming marshmallow man will quiver like Jell-O. Remember, it's hot, so don't let the kids touch it until it totally cools.

Teaching the Lesson

At first, when the marshmallow man started plumping up, the marshmallows actually seemed okay. But the longer we left the marshmallows in the microwave, the worse they got. This cute little marshmallow man isn't cute anymore. We've destroyed it.

A similar thing happens in life. Sometimes we get in the spotlight somehow, just like our little marshmallow man was in the light of this microwave. Maybe people tell us what a great job we did and some pride swells up inside us. We need to remember that while that feels good at first, we can get puffed up with pride and destroy ourselves too.

The Bible is full of stories of those who were hurt or destroyed by their own pride. Can anybody tell us of one?

- **Satan.** Pride was his undoing.
- **King Saul.** The women shouting, "Saul has killed his thousands, David his ten thousands" hit a nerve with Saul. His pride drove him into murderous jealousy.
- **Solomon** thought he was so wise he could bend the rules a bit and build temples for the gods of his many wives. He was proud and didn't think it would have any effect on his own dedication to God. He totally miscalculated.
- **Samson.** His pride in his strength and ability to escape his enemies blinded him a bit, which led to his capture and the enemy permanently blinding him.
- **Pharisees.** They were puffed up with a sense of their own self-importance—to their own destruction. They wouldn't even consider Jesus was who he

claimed to be, and these leaders wanted to hang on to the spotlight themselves. A definite strategic error.

Let's look at some Scripture.

> Pride leads to disgrace,
> but with humility comes wisdom. (Prov. 11:2 NLT)

> Pride goes before destruction,
> a haughty spirit before a fall. (16:18)

- When we're proud, we see ourselves as the most important person in the room. How can that lead to mistakes, sin, and trouble?
- When we're proud, we aren't as open to instruction, advice, or constructive criticism. How can that lead to mistakes, sin, and trouble?
- When we're proud, it is easier to get angry. "How dare they do that to *me*?" How can that lead to mistakes, sin, and trouble?
- When we're proud, we feel entitled and like we're an exception to the rules. How can that lead to mistakes, sin, and trouble?

Pride, left unchecked, is a destroyer. Sometimes Dad or Mom may say something like this to you: "I'm so proud of you," "You did a great job," or, "You should be proud of yourself."

The thing is if you really do that . . . if you get filled with pride about something you did or accomplished, you'll be on your way to destroying yourself. When Dad or Mom, or anyone else, tells you how proud they are of you, or tells you that you should be proud of yourself, you need to remember who really deserves the credit.

- Who gave you the opportunity?
- Who gave you the ability?
- Who gave you life in the first place and the health to live it?
- Who really deserves all the credit?

When we start thinking we're big stuff instead of giving God the thanks and credit, we're headed for trouble.

Acts 12:21–23 tells the story of Herod and what happened to him when he just absorbed the praise people gave him instead of directing it to God, where it belonged.

> On the appointed day Herod, wearing his royal robes, sat on his throne and delivered a public address to the people. They shouted, "This is the voice of a god, not of a man." Immediately, because Herod did not give praise to God, an angel of the Lord struck him down, and he was eaten by worms and died.

God doesn't mess around with pride. Herod's pride led to his downfall, and it happened fast. Whether fast or slow, pride will destroy us.

Even Jesus made sure that God got the praise when he did something spectacular. Check out the story in Mark 2:1–13 in which Jesus healed the paralyzed man who was lowered through a roof by friends. After the healing, the people left praising God, not Jesus.

Summing It Up

Take a look at the marshmallow man. He's deflated and looks pitiful, right? Remember, that is what happens when we get puffed up with pride.

> Pride brings a person low,
>   but the lowly in spirit gain honor. (Prov. 29:23)

When we're feeling proud, we need to quickly turn that into praise for God. We need to thank him. Acknowledge him. And by doing that we'll avoid the destructive effects of pride.

> In the same way, you who are younger, submit yourselves to your elders. All of you, clothe yourselves with humility toward one another, because,
>
> > "God opposes the proud
> > but shows favor to the humble."
>
> Humble yourselves, therefore, under God's mighty hand, that he may lift you up in due time. (1 Pet. 5:5–6)

A Real Slimeball

+12 THINGS YOU'LL NEED

You can search online for "easy slime recipe" and get plenty of ideas for slime. Or you can use the one I describe below.

If making slime is out of the question, you can always buy ready-made slime. Just know it's pricier that way—especially since you'll want to have slime for each of the kids.

☐ Elmer's white glue

☐ 20 Mule Team Borax (available in the detergent aisle of most grocery stores)

☐ Food coloring (optional)

☐ Measuring cups (¼ cup and ½ cup)

☐ 2-liter bottle

☐ Eyedropper (optional)

- ☐ Stir stick or pencil
- ☐ Disposable plastic cups

KEEP IT SAFE

Most slime recipes are toxic. Glue is a main ingredient—and you definitely don't want your kids eating glue. Common sense, right? But I had to say it.

Advance Prep

You've read the theme. This is a really uncomfortable topic, but as a parent, you're all about protecting your kids. And the best time to warn your kids about people who "use" others for their own selfish motives is now—if your kids are age appropriate. If some of your kids are the right age but others are a little young, be sure to take the older ones aside and go over this. Don't wait until the younger ones are ready so you can teach them all together.

If you have boys, you'll also want to warn them about becoming slimeballs themselves—or hanging with friends who are.

Ultimately, you want to give them just a taste of the kind of person a guy should be on a date.

Now, some men will shy away from the topic because they were a bit of a slimeball themselves in their dating years. If that's you, I'm going to guess you've done a lot of changing since then. As a parent, you've got to get past your past. Your job now is to protect your kids. Whether or not you "did it right" in your dating years, you must talk to your kids about how to do it right. Failing to warn and protect your kids would be a tragedy.

You'll have two things to do ahead of time to prepare for this lesson.

- First, pick up the ingredients to make the slime with the kids. It would be great if you could make a trial batch in advance if you've got the time, just so you know what you're doing when it comes time for the kids to be involved.
- Second, read the story in 2 Samuel 13:1–21 so you can be thinking about it a bit. Don't wait to read and digest it for the first time while you're trying to teach the devotional to the kids.

To make the slime:

- Mix equal volumes of glue and water in a disposable cup. Whatever size batch you make, keep that glue-to-water ratio at 1:1. Keep in mind that when you do this with the kids, you'll want to make enough slime for each of them to enjoy. Better yet, let each of the kids make their own batch. While you're testing this slime recipe out in advance, I'd suggest mixing ¼ cup of glue with ¼ cup of water. That's an easy amount to handle.
- If you want to add some food coloring, this is the time to do that.
- Stir the solution thoroughly.
- Mix your Borax solution. Take the label off the 2-liter bottle. Clearly relabel the bottle as Borax. Now fill the bottle halfway with water and add ½ cup of Borax. Stir vigorously for several minutes, but realize the Borax may not dissolve right away.
- Pour off a couple of ounces of the Borax solution into an empty cup. Now, if you have an eyedropper, this is when you'll want to use it. The eyedropper allows you to add just a tiny bit of this Borax solution at a time to the glue/water mix. If you add too much of the Borax solution, the slime will become really stiff.
- Use the stir stick to mix the glue/water mixture with the Borax solution. The solution will glom on the stick, so at some point you'll want to wipe off the stick with your finger.
- Now work the solution in your hands to bring it the rest of the way.

Now you can play with the slime—and store it in a plastic bag if you'd like to keep it.

Running the Activity

The activity here is making the slime with the kids—letting them play with it a bit. If you'd rather make the slime in advance so it's ready to play with when you get the kids together, that works too.

Sit the kids around the table, scoop them each some slime, and let them play with the goopy stuff a bit. No other specific instructions are needed here.

- You have kids.
- They have slime.
- You won't need to tell them what to do.

After a few minutes of them playing with it, start teaching the lesson. The slime will keep their hands busy as you talk.

Teaching the Lesson

Messing with the slime is fun, right? Slime has a way of drawing us to it. It's almost like we can't help ourselves.

Sometimes we refer to certain types of guys as "slimeballs." It has nothing to do with their personal hygiene. The type of person I'm referring to may be attractive. Charming. Interesting. Fun. They may be seen as popular or the life of the party. In a way, they're magnetic . . . and girls are drawn to them. But slimeballs have a dark side to them too. Slimeballs are all about using girls to satisfy their own lust or selfish desires. Slimeballs are dangerous guys—and we want to warn you to stay far away from them.

What are some characteristics of a guy who is a slimeball?

- He's often smooth. He's complimentary and charming, but only because he knows that's the best way to get what he wants.
- He appears to care about you. He acts interested in what you're interested in.
- He comes across like you can trust him, but deep inside you may sense that something is off.

- He's manipulative and controlling but can do it in a nice way—at least at first. He will tell you whatever he thinks you need to hear so that he can take advantage of you. It could swing from telling you how much he cares to making you feel guilty if you don't show him how much you care for him. Generally, he wants that shown in a physical/sexual way.

- His personal wants and needs drive him. Often, this is nothing more than lust. A thirst for thrills—at someone else's expense.

- He sees everything he spends on you—time, attention, money—as an *investment*. And he expects a return on that investment in a physical/sexual way.

- He lacks honor and integrity. He puts his wants above everything—and everyone else—which is why he will use a girl. A guy of true honor and integrity should respect and protect a girl.

There are a number of slimeballs described in the Bible. Let's look at the story of Amnon, a classic slimeball, by reading 2 Samuel 13:1–22.

- Amnon wanted sex, wasn't willing to wait for marriage, and raped his half sister to get it.

- Amnon didn't respect Tamar, who was a daughter of King David.

- Amnon used deception and lies to get Tamar to lower her guard. He pretended to be sick to get her to his bed . . . to get her where he wanted her.

- When Amnon was done with her, he treated her like trash. And often this is exactly what slimeballs do. After they get what they want from a girl, they treat the girl like garbage.

There was more than one slimeball in the story.

Did you catch it? Amnon's friend and cousin, Jonadab, helped come up with the plan to lure Tamar into Amnon's bedroom.

- Was Jonadab doing what was best for Tamar? Hardly.

- Was Jonadab really, truly a good friend to Amnon—by helping him sin like that?

Any friend who encourages you to do something wrong is not a good friend at all. Jonadab was looking out for his own interests. And we see this even more later in the story. In 2 Samuel 13:32–33, Jonadab reveals that he was aware of a plot to kill Amnon.

- Yet he never warned Amnon—his cousin and so-called friend.
- And Jonadab never told King David—who could have prevented the murder.

Yeah, Jonadab was a total slimeball.

How should a guy treat a girl on a date?

There are many things that can be said here, but let me highlight a few.

- A guy must remember that any girl he takes out is a daughter of the King.
- A guy should be the girl's protector on the date. He keeps her safe from harm—emotional and physical.
- A guy doesn't step over the line physically with his date, no matter how bad he wants to, how much others convince him it's okay, or even if the girl is willing. He doesn't sin against God or the girl—and doesn't lead the girl into sinning against God. He follows God's guidelines, which means no inappropriate touching or sex before marriage.

Slime can be entertaining, but in the long run, it's pretty useless. You can't build anything lasting with it. In fact, slime doesn't make anything stronger. If you use slime to glue something together, it will disappoint you every time.

Slimeballs can be the same way. They may impress you at first. They may be entertaining. They may be the life of the party. But in the long run, they're not the kind of person who builds good, strong, lasting relationships.

Summing It Up

Messing with slime can be fun . . . but stay away from guys who are slimeballs.

- Girls, avoid guys who are slimeballs, no matter how attractive or magnetic you think they are. They are users and abusers. They'll hurt you and your future.
- Guys, don't be a slimeball. Commit yourself to be a protector . . . always. And stay away from slimeball friends who encourage you to do wrong things with or to girls.

A Special Word for Parents

Keep your antenna up. Chances are one of your kids may need a little one-on-one follow-up about an issue you raised. Talk to them when they're more likely to be open. If you're talking to your son, food is always a good idea. Guys talk better when they're eating—or doing something other than just sitting uncomfortably across from you. And both sons and daughters will likely talk more if it is late at night in a dark room. I know—that's exactly when you want to hit the sack and get some rest, but you're the protector here. Talk to them when you have the greatest chance of them opening up.

And while you're talking to them, if they confess something that they did . . . be quick to listen, slow to speak, and slow to get angry. Sounds kind of like James 1:19–20, doesn't it? Remember, they need your help. Kids often make really poor judgments. So take a moment to pray and ask God to help you respond well. How you react to your son or daughter will likely determine if they'll open up to you again.

Fast Freeze

Hard hearts lead to shattered lives

 ## THINGS YOU'LL NEED

- ☐ Dry ice, at least five pounds. I usually get it at a supermarket. Google "dry ice" and you'll find places that sell it in your area. Air makes dry ice evaporate quickly, so I take towels to wrap it in and then put it in a cooler to bring it home. You'll want to pick up the dry ice just before you do the experiment. Realize that dry ice is at –109 degrees, which means that even storing it in your freezer is like keeping it in a hot car in the summer. A freezer is over 130 degrees *warmer* than the dry ice.

- ☐ Heavy-duty rubber gloves, available at your local hardware store. Get the ones that are chemical resistant.

- ☐ Steel hammer (a big rubber mallet is also nice as an addition, but it is optional)

- ☐ Scrap of plywood or cutting board to protect table when hammering

- [ ] Acetone (a quart), often found in the paint section of your hardware store
- [ ] Dowel to use as a stir stick, or use the handle of a wooden spoon
- [ ] Glass container. I use a 500ml beaker, but you can use a wide-mouth glass jar or a thick glass bowl.
- [ ] Tongs
- [ ] Hot dogs
- [ ] Small dill pickles (whole)
- [ ] Bath towel (not your best one—you may damage it)
- [ ] Safety glasses for all present (you and the kids)
- [ ] Grill or shop apron—or older clothes. If the acetone splatters, it may remove color.

Advance Prep

You're going to make a supercold slush so you can fast-freeze a hot dog and a pickle. It'll be an unforgettable way to talk about hard hearts. Don't let the detailed list of supplies cause you to skip this lesson. This isn't hard to do, and it's a great lesson—one you and your kids will love.

As always, you're best off doing a trial run ahead of time. If you have older kids, let them in on it so they can help. They'll feel special, and they definitely won't mind doing this one twice. Be sure to put the safety glasses, apron, and gloves on *before* you start.

1. Put the dry ice on the towel, then fold the towel over to cover the dry ice.
2. Take the hammer and pound the dry ice to break it down. The goal is to pound it down to a frozen powder, about the consistency of course sand. The towel keeps the dry ice in place while you pound. After maybe thirty seconds of pounding, I switch over to a big rubber mallet to grind the dry ice up a little finer.
3. Pour some acetone into the glass container. Start with roughly four ounces. It's easier to add more later.

4. Now scoop up the dry ice powder and add it to the acetone. You'll get a nice blast of vapor as the two meet—which is another reason why you're wearing safety glasses.

5. Use the dowel to mix the acetone / dry ice powder into a slushy solution. Add dry ice powder or acetone as needed to get the consistency right.

6. Add a hot dog and a pickle or two. Bury them in the solution, adding more dry ice powder and acetone if necessary to be sure the pickle and hot dog are covered completely.

7. Set a timer for two minutes, and when the time is up, use the tongs to dig out the hot dog and pickle.

8. Place the hot dog / pickle on a hard, protected surface (some scrap plywood or a cutting board) and give each one a whack with the hammer (not the rubber mallet). They'll shatter, sending shrapnel everywhere.

Also, as part of your prep, read a few chapters of Exodus, starting at chapter 7, and circle all the times the Bible mentions Pharaoh's heart being hard (7:3; 7:13–14; 7:22; 8:15; 8:19; 8:32; 9:7; 9:12; 9:34; 10:20; 10:27).

Running the Activity

Make sure everyone in the room is wearing safety glasses/gear before you start. Then make the fast-freeze slushy solution just like you practiced—but with the kids helping this time.

While you're working together . . .

- Explain just how cold the solution you're making is compared to a traditional freezer. The freeze point of acetone is even colder than dry ice, which explains why the solution doesn't freeze in the container.

- Have one of the kids set the timer for two minutes after you add the hot dog and pickle.

- Explain how combining the right ingredients creates a solution that will freeze things rock-solid in just a minute or two. Pliable things like hot dogs and pickles become rigid. Something that normally bends will break. Something that would normally shake will shatter.

When the two minutes are up, use the tongs to remove the pickle and hot dog, and place them on the plywood or cutting board. Give the kids turns at shattering them by hitting them with a steel hammer.

Teaching the Lesson

Hardening pickles and hot dogs in this fast-freeze solution can be fun, but there's a very chilling parallel to the Christian life. The Bible warns about a deadly hardness that can creep into us—and it can happen quickly. I'm talking about the danger of developing a hard heart.

Remember the story of the exodus, when the Israelites were freed from slavery in Egypt? The Bible tells us repeatedly that Pharaoh had a hard heart, or that he hardened his heart, and that in some cases God hardened Pharaoh's heart. I've circled some of those times in my Bible (flip through the pages to show them).

Pharaoh, under the influence of his hard heart, made horrible decisions that led to pain and suffering and loss for himself and his entire nation. Again and again Pharaoh had a chance to do the right thing, and multiple times he was warned about what would happen if he didn't, but his hard heart stubbornly kept making poor choices.

Even after God hit Egypt with plagues of blood, frogs, and gnats, Pharaoh still resisted obeying God (Exod. 8:18–19). Pharaoh's magicians were spooked. They knew God was real, powerful—and determined. They tried to get Pharaoh to see that. But here we see part of the truth of having a hard heart. People with hard hearts are blind to the obvious and don't listen to reason—to their own hurt.

First John 2:9–11 shows us that a person with a hard heart is in darkness and can't see their way.

- How might your life go badly if you don't listen to reason, miss the obvious, make bad decisions, and can't see your way?

How does someone get a hard heart?

A look at King Nebuchadnezzar in the Old Testament reveals two things that combine to make hard hearts: pride and disobedience to God.

Daniel tells of King Nebuchadnezzar's hard heart.

But when his heart became arrogant and hardened with pride, he was deposed from his royal throne and stripped of his glory. (Dan. 5:20)

Daniel had warned Nebuchadnezzar to turn away from what he was doing wrong. But Nebuchadnezzar continued to do things that were wrong and did not follow God's obvious commands, even though he knew better.

When you combine *pride* and *willful disobedience*, ignoring God's Word and having a sense that *I'm entitled to special rules just for me*, you create a heart that is cold and hard. And it doesn't take long. A heart can harden in minutes too.

Haven't you felt your own heart go hard when you're having a disagreement with someone? In Mark 10:5, Jesus points out that even the root of divorce boils down to one issue: hard hearts. This is serious stuff. Hard hearts destroy relationships between people.

- Do you think Pharaoh or King Nebuchadnezzar knew their heart was hard?
- Is it possible that our hearts might be hard in some way too—without us fully being aware of it?

What might be some symptoms of your own heart getting hard?

- Where you were once *pliable*, you become *immovable*.
- Where you were once *flexible*, you become *rigid*.
- Where you were once *caring*, you become *insensitive*.
- Where you were once *moved*, you're filled with *apathy*.
- Where you were once *convicted*, you feel *no shame*.
- Where you were once *kind*, you become *rude* and *critical*.
- Where you were once *patient*, you become *short* and *irritated*.
- Where you once sought to *understand others*, you *argue your position*.
- Where you once sought to *please God*, you now try to *please yourself*.

None of you would hold your finger in this slushy solution for two minutes. That's crazy. Dangerous. You'd kill your finger . . . after two minutes, you could probably just snap it off. If you dipped your finger in this solution, you'd get it out of there immediately.

Hard-heartedness in our lives is just as dangerous. We must guard against it in our lives.

How do we soften a hard heart?

If we know that pride and disobedience help cause hard hearts, it makes sense that we confess them.

- Ask God to open our eyes and soften our hearts.
- Give the Holy Spirit permission to change us.

I know this works, because God has softened my hard heart many times.

Summing It Up

Hebrews 3:12–15 talks about the Israelites when they were on the edge of the promised land . . . a land they were to conquer. But it looked tough. Impossible. Somehow, they forgot that the job was really in God's hands.

- In their pride, they felt the job of conquering was all up to them.
- In their pride, they failed to remember how God had protected them in the desert.
- They disobeyed God's clear command to go in and conquer the land.

And as a result of their pride and disobedience, their hearts hardened. And like Pharaoh, they lost big. God didn't allow that generation into the promised land. They missed out on God's best for their lives.

- Pride and willful disobedience to God's Word combine to create hard hearts.
- People with hard hearts don't see clearly. They miss the obvious.
- They make bad decisions that hurt themselves and others.
- People with hard hearts miss God's best for them.

Hard hearts are dangerous. Deadly. Let's be sure we're on guard against them.

Watermelon Drop

THEME: Holding on to purity, integrity, honoring parents, honoring God, and staying true to our faith

THINGS YOU'LL NEED

- ☐ Six watermelons (can substitute eggs)
- ☐ Permanent marker
- ☐ Step ladder or second-story window to drop watermelons from
- ☐ Plastic sheeting (if doing this indoors)

Advance Prep

You're going to drop the watermelons/eggs from a high enough position to ensure that they smash, so you'll need to decide on the site for your launch pad. A second-story window would be ideal. Or you could use a step ladder to get the height you need. Once I stood on the flat roof of the church and dropped the watermelons onto the parking lot. It was better than fireworks. I've also dropped eggs from shoulder height when we needed to contain the mess a bit more.

During the lesson, you can drop the watermelons—or let the kids do it. I've done the lesson both ways. Either the kids have the joy of dropping them or the fun of standing near the impact zone.

Dropping the watermelons on a hard surface is important. So if there is grass below the window, drag a piece of plywood to the drop zone so the watermelons are sure to splatter on impact.

I'm going to go forward with this lesson as if you're using watermelons, but you can use raw eggs if you'd prefer. They cost less, are always in season, and make less mess—but they don't make quite the "splash" that a watermelon makes. If you use eggs, you can definitely do this lesson indoors too, if you spread a little plastic.

Take the permanent marker and write a different word or phrase across each watermelon in bold letters: PURITY, INTEGRITY, HONORING PARENTS, HONORING GOD, STAYING TRUE TO THE FAITH, or whatever else you'd like to emphasize. Keep one watermelon blank.

And during the activity with the kids, it would be great to shoot a video—in slow-mo. The kids will enjoy watching it later—and it will make a great reminder for the truth of the lesson.

Running the Activity

Have the row of watermelons lined up so the words written on them are visible. Keep the blank watermelon out of sight for now.

There are many things we've been taught to hold on to. Things we're to protect. Here are a few.

- **Purity.** Staying free from a secret life of getting into porn, for example. Avoiding physical acts of sex before marriage.

- **Integrity.** Being honest. Trustworthy. Dependable. Kind. Doing the right things.

- **Honoring parents** by being obedient and respectful. By obeying us . . . even when we wouldn't know if you didn't. By not complaining about having to obey us.

- **Honoring God** by obeying him and clinging to him. By living according to God's Word.
- **Staying true to the faith.** We don't put on an act and become a hypocrite, and our personal faith in God is real, growing, and showing fruit in our lives.

We know these things are important. The Bible says they are. But the enemy wants you to relax your convictions. The enemy wants you to let them go. Sometimes friends will encourage you to let them go too. They'll try to convince you of how much fun it will be.

But when you let these virtues drop, what happens?

Each of you grab a watermelon, and let's find out.

Have each of the kids grab a watermelon and carry it out to the launch site. If you're on the second story, bring all the watermelons to the second floor and then send the kids down to wait on the ground below. They'll appreciate how the watermelons burst at the moment of impact.

(Before each watermelon is dropped, read its label and remind them of how the world is going to urge them to let that go.)

This watermelon represents *purity*. The Word says you're to hang on to it, but the world and maybe some of your friends may encourage you to let it go. Let's see what happens when we do.

(Repeat this procedure before you drop each watermelon. I'd wait until after you teach the lesson before you clean up the mess so you don't lose their attention.)

Teaching the Lesson

Purity. Integrity. Honoring parents. Honoring God. Staying true to the faith. Each of these, and more, are things the Bible tells us to hang on to. And with each of these, you'll have the world and friends trying to convince you that you'll miss something fun and exciting if you *don't* let them go.

- Do you think it might be fun, exciting, and sometimes thrilling to let some of these go?

- Do you think your friends might accept you better if you let some of these go?
- Ultimately, who would you let down . . . who would be disappointed if you let one or more of these go?

The Bible says this in John 10:10:

> The thief comes only to steal and kill and destroy; I have come that they may have life, and have it to the full.

This pretty well sums up what our enemy—the devil and his demons—is all about. It sounds like something right out of a horror film. Steal. Kill. Destroy.

- **Steal**—your true joy, and leave you with crippling guilt and shame and consequences. Steal your future joy too, especially when it comes to purity.
- **Kill**—your passion for God and for following him. When we sin, something inside us dies. And this often leads to a whole lot more compromise and pain.
- **Destroy**—your purpose, some of the very things God has planned for you to do and to accomplish here on earth. See Ephesians 2:10.

There is so much more that I can say about this topic—and if you want to keep talking about it, we can. Otherwise, let me start to sum this up.

Summing It Up

God makes it clear that we're to hang on to some things. Guard them. But it can be really tempting to drop those things. Friends can pressure us to let them go too. It can bring short-term thrills. It can be fun. But like smashing watermelons, letting go of things God tells us to cling to always leaves a mess.

And some things, like virginity, you can never get back once you've let them go.

Sin is sticky. The effects of it tend to stay around a long time, and the consequences in the future can be really costly.

When we get something sticky on our hands, other dirt and junk tends to stick to them as well. Sin works the same way. When we don't keep our hands clean from sin, more and more tends to cling to us. (Pull out the one watermelon you didn't write on, the one you didn't drop. Use that as a visual as you remind them not to let these key areas in their lives "drop.")

The Word tells us to hang on to some things.

- Purity . . . always. The day will come when you will enjoy sex in marriage, but the enemy wants to offer you a shortcut.
- Integrity . . . always. Honest + truthful
- Honoring parents . . . always. Of course, we're working toward you being free and making all your own decisions, but honoring parents is something you'll do for your lifetime, and someday you'll have kids who do the same.
- Honoring God . . . always.
- Staying true to the faith . . . always, always, always.

Don't let them go. Cling to them. Protect them—even when it would be easy to let them go. Make sense?

I think we would all say that we love God, or that we want to love him. This is a way you can show you truly love. Trust God enough to obey him and live his way.

Love must be sincere. Hate what is evil; cling to what is good. (Rom. 12:9)

Do not be overcome by evil, but overcome evil with good. (v. 21)

Have the kids help you clean up the debris—a subtle reminder that sin makes a mess. Also, cut up that good watermelon, the one you didn't drop, so everyone can have a snack. It will be one more reminder that holding on to the things God tells us to cling to can actually bring us nourishment and enjoyment in the future.

Brain Food

THINGS YOU'LL NEED

- [ ] Jell-O mold. This can be round to represent a brain, or better yet, see lesson 17 for where to find a brain-shaped Jell-O mold.

- [ ] Enough boxes of Jell-O to fill the mold you choose—twice. You're going to make two Jell-O molds. Try to pick the flavor your kids will like the very best, *but you want it to be clear enough that the kids can see into it.*

- [ ] Nasty stuff to put in one of the Jell-O molds as you're making it. A big handful of debris from a vacuum bag. Hair from a hairbrush. Dirt. Gravel. Real bugs or flies (dead). If you go with plastic bugs from a toy store, realize they will tend to float, so you'll need to adjust. Go to the grocery store and buy sardines or a fish. Wouldn't a fish head look great in your Jell-O? The more gross stuff you can fit in that Jell-O, the better.

- ☐ Two plates
- ☐ Two sets of clean bowls and spoons for you and the kids
- ☐ Two serving spoons to scoop the Jell-O

Advance Prep

Make the two Jell-O molds in advance. You'll need time for them to solidify. You may want to have one of the older kids help you with this, but that's your call.

Make one Jell-O perfectly—and be sure it's their favorite flavor.

Make the second one with all the nasty stuff that you can fit in it. Put some of the junk (like the fish) near the edges so it is more visible.

After the Jell-O has set, gently remove it from the mold and set your masterpieces each on a separate plate.

Running the Activity

(Hide the perfect Jell-O, and have only the nasty one on the table when you call in the kids for the lesson.) Can you see the shadows of the junk inside? Perfect. Have a clean bowl and spoon set out for each of the kids. And when they sit down around the table, show them the brain-shaped Jell-O and scoop a bowl for each of them. Make sure that each of the kids has noticeable nasty stuff in their portion.

Teaching the Lesson

I've made a very special brain Jell-O for you to enjoy. What do you think?

Okay, so I see you're not too eager to eat the Jell-O. The hair, dirt, fish, bugs—none of these actually belong in Jell-O. It isn't appetizing when you put this nasty stuff in it. It isn't appealing.

This Jell-O represents our brains. God wants us to keep them good and pure, but sometimes we put things in our brains that don't belong there. Can you give me some examples?

- **Movies, music, books, and video games.** Are we feeding junk into our brains—things that don't belong in Christians?
- **Drugs and alcohol.** This stuff alters our brain chemistry, certainly for the short term—and sometimes for the long run too.
- **Pornography.** This changes our brain chemistry—and doesn't belong in our brains.
- **Bad influences.** Whether in person or through media, the Bible warns that bad company corrupts good morals. How are these influences adding things to us that shouldn't be part of a Christian's life?
- **Attitudes.** Selfishness. Pride. A sense of entitlement. All these and more don't belong in our brains.

Okay, so when I was making the Jell-O, I allowed some bad things to go into it. Now, when it comes time to use the Jell-O for the very thing it was created—to bring enjoyment to me and those I love—it doesn't work so well.

The stuff we allow in our heads—the things we put in our brains—tends to stay there, just like the junk I put in the Jell-O. It doesn't magically disappear. And the stuff tends to come out. Even the things we hide. But that isn't even the worst of it. When it comes time for God to use us in the ways he's planned to use us, we may not be so useable. That's a scary thought.

Summing It Up

(Pull out the good Jell-O, clean bowls, spoons, and serving spoon. Give each of the kids a bowl of the good Jell-O.) Now this is the way Jell-O is supposed to be. Good. Clean. Refreshing. And that's what God wants for us too.

This Jell-O is appetizing. The other Jell-O? Not so much. In life, sometimes we think we need to be like the kids who sneak and watch things they shouldn't. We are tempted to fill our minds with junk just like they do. Remember, those other kids are actually hurting themselves. The nasty stuff people put in their brains stays there—and tends to come out eventually.

Just like this pure, clean Jell-O, the person who sets themselves apart for God—to do things right—is going to be the appetizing one, the one others will really want to be around in the long run. The person who sets themselves apart for God will be ready to do what God created them to do—bring him glory and enjoyment and show God's love to others.

Guard your minds. Be careful what you let your eyes see, ears hear, and so on, and you'll be more pleasing to God and to others because of it. It's a no-brainer.

> Hold on to instruction, do not let it go;
>> guard it well, for it is your life.
> Do not set foot on the path of the wicked
>> or walk in the way of evildoers.
> Avoid it, do not travel on it;
>> turn from it and go on your way. (Prov. 4:13–15)

> Above all else, guard your heart,
>> for everything you do flows from it. (v. 23)

Finally, brothers and sisters, whatever is true, whatever is noble, whatever is right, whatever is pure, whatever is lovely, whatever is admirable—if anything is excellent or praiseworthy—think about such things. Whatever you have learned or received or heard from me, or seen in me—put into practice. And the God of peace will be with you. (Phil. 4:8–9)

Easy Target

Going to church helps us stay on fire for Christ . . . avoiding church makes our passion easier to extinguish

THINGS YOU'LL NEED

- ☐ Squirt gun / water pistol for each of the kids. You're *not* looking for a high-powered, super-soaker type. In this case, something smaller is better.
- ☐ Fire pit or campfire—and everything that goes with that. Logs, starting fluid, and matches or a lighter. You'll want at least one log to be smaller, maybe the size of your wrist.
- ☐ Fireplace poker, tongs, or fireproof gloves—really anything that will allow you to remove one small log from the fire.
- ☐ Stopwatch (such as the one on your smartphone)

Advance Prep

If you have the chance to practice this in advance, great. Running through it one time will make the activity go smoother when you do it with the kids. And it will also ensure that you have the right squirt guns for the job. You don't want ones that will douse the fire too quickly—or ones that will take forever to extinguish it either.

Your goal is to show the kids that a log in a fire pit or campfire is a lot harder to extinguish than one that is separated from the others.

Running the Activity

After your fire is strong and blazing, you're ready to begin the lesson.

- Separate one log—about the size of your wrist—from the fire pit or campfire.
- Give each of your kids a squirt gun, and using the stopwatch, time how long it takes them to extinguish that log you pulled from the fire. When they're done, there should be no visible flames on that log. It may still be smoking—and that's fine.
- Now put that log back in the fire with the rest of the logs and let it fully reignite while you refill the squirt guns.
- Ask the kids to extinguish the same log again—but this time while it's in the fire with the other logs. Allow them only the same amount of time they had when they extinguished it the first time (if you are using your phone, set the timer to the exact number of seconds it took to extinguish the log the first time).
- When the time is up, the kids must stop squirting.

As long as the squirt guns you're using aren't too big, likely your kids won't be able to extinguish the flame while the log is with all the other burning ones. That's exactly the result you're looking for.

Teaching the Lesson

When the log was separated from the others, it was easy to extinguish. After the log was returned to the fire and reignited, its fire was much more difficult to put out, right?

We did this to illustrate an important truth about Christians and the church today.

Sometimes when someone is really serious about their faith—about obeying God's Word, following his ways, and loving God—we might refer to them as being "on fire."

- Do you think that a Christian who is "on fire" is one who becomes a target of the devil and his demons?

- Do you think they seek to extinguish that Christian's burning desire to follow God?

- Do you suppose it would be easier to quench that Christian's dedication to God if that Christian were off on their own somewhere—or in a church surrounded by other solid believers?

- Because of school, sports, work, or just life, sometimes Christians don't make it to church every week. There has been a growing trend of redefining "regular" church attendance as being something less than it traditionally used to be. Sometimes a person who claims to be a regular church attender may go to church only once or twice a month. How might that make them an easier target for the enemy?

Listen to this verse:

And let us consider how we may spur one another on toward love and good deeds, not giving up meeting together, as some are in the habit of doing, but encouraging one another—and all the more as you see the Day approaching. (Heb. 10:24–25)

When this verse talks about the "Day," it is referring to a day in the future—when Jesus comes back.

- Are we closer to Jesus's return today than we were last year?

- What does the verse say? The closer and closer we get to that day, are we to be dedicated to getting to church with other believers more and more—or less and less?

- Why do you think God emphasizes in his Word that we need to be more dedicated to getting to church and being with other believers the closer we get to Jesus coming back?

- What does that suggest about some of the activities and things that keep us from getting to church?

Summing It Up

The closer we get to Jesus's return, likely the more intense the efforts will be on the part of the devil and his demons to extinguish our dedication to God. The devil and his demons are running out of time—and they know it. So it only makes sense that they're dialing up their efforts to keep us from church and from burning strong for God. If our burning desire to live for God weakens, we'll be the ones who suffer.

And if we're not in church, we won't be there to urge one another on to love others and to do good. We won't be there to encourage others.

Going to church weekly and being surrounded by other believers is a really good way to help keep our flame burning strong—and for us to help others keep burning strong as well. It is no wonder that God wants us to get to church—to be with other believers more and more as the enemy steps up efforts to extinguish our flame. Like we saw with the fire and squirt guns, we're a much easier target when we're separated from other believers.

Sometimes the less we get together with other believers for the purpose of strengthening our walk with the Lord, the more our relationship with God begins to cool. And often the sense of urgency to be with other believers cools down too. Let's do all we can to keep that from happening to us. Let's do all we can to follow God's Word—and stay burning for God in the process.

Get a Grip

THEME: Keep your hands "clean" if you want to have a good grip on the Christian life

THINGS YOU'LL NEED

- ☐ 18- to 24-inch length of 3-inch PVC pipe
- ☐ 5-foot length of rope
- ☐ Drill and bit (optional, used to attach rope to PVC)
- ☐ Bottle of hand lotion
- ☐ Gallon jug of water
- ☐ Hand towels for cleanup

Advance Prep

Keep in mind that you'll likely drip gobs of lotion on the floor, so you won't want to do this over carpet.

- Attach one end of the rope securely to the PVC. You can either tie it around the midpoint of the length of the PVC or, better yet, drill a hole through the PVC at the center and thread the rope through before tying a knot in the end. You'll be winding the rope around the PVC, and it is important that the rope doesn't slip.
- Tie the other end of the rope to the handle of a gallon jug of water.
- Hold the PVC ends in an overhand grip, with the PVC parallel to the ground. With arms extended, keeping the PVC at about shoulder height, wind the gallon of water up toward the PVC. The rope should wrap neatly around the center of the PVC, leaving the ends clear. Easy, right?
- Now, lower the gallon and do it again—but this time you're going to slather your hands with lotion first. If you keep your hands on the PVC, it will be nearly impossible to wind up the gallon this time.

Use a towel to clean up the PVC, and you're ready to do this with the kids.

Running the Activity

Demonstrate how you'd like the gallon of water raised by winding the rope like you practiced. Then ask for a volunteer to take a turn rolling it up.

- Once they've successfully raised the gallon, ask them to lower it.
- Now ask your volunteer to hold their hands out with their palms up.
- Pull out the lotion and generously glom some on each hand. Use lots of it. Have them rub their palms together to make sure the lotion has full coverage.
- Ask them to wind up the gallon of water like they did the first time.

Obviously, they're going to have big problems doing that. Perfect.

Teaching the Lesson

Winding up the gallon the first time, when your hands were clean, was a little tricky—but you could do it, right? But the second time—when I added all that lotion to your hands and your hands weren't clean—it was impossible.

- As Christians, we can choose to live with "clean hands" or "dirty hands." Anybody want to take a stab at explaining what I mean by that?

- What kinds of sin might leave us with "dirty hands" as Christians?

- Would being selfish or proud or unkind or unforgiving give us dirty hands?

- Winding up the gallon of water was nearly impossible without clean hands. How might we make our lives more difficult if we don't keep our hands clean—if we don't work at living as a Christian should?

- How might living like "It's all about me" make life more difficult?

- How might failing to curb our pride make life more difficult?

- How would living a double life—acting like a Christian in front of our parents, for example, but behaving very differently when around others—make life more difficult?

- How would getting sloppy with how we obey God's Word make life more difficult?

- How would breaking God's guidelines for living sexually pure make life more difficult?

Not only will we complicate our lives when we don't keep our hands clean but we'll also sabotage our ability to help others.

Imagine this isn't a gallon of water on the end of the rope but a friend of yours. And they're hanging off the Golden Gate Bridge. The only thing that is keeping them from falling into the San Francisco Bay far below them is this PVC contraption—and you're holding it. You may not be able to winch them up with your bare hands until help arrives, but if your hands aren't clean, will you even be able to hold on to them at all?

In life, we're to be an example to believers and unbelievers of what a Christian is all about. Imagine that gallon of water being the gospel . . . the "Living Water" Jesus talked about. If we don't have "clean hands," we aren't going to be effective holding that gospel out to others at all. We won't be a good example—and we won't be able to help others like we should.

Let's look at a couple verses.

Live clean, innocent lives as children of God, shining like bright lights in a world full of crooked and perverse people. Hold firmly to the word of life; then, on the day of Christ's return, I will be proud that I did not run the race in vain and that my work was not useless. (Phil. 2:15–16 NLT)

Our entire lives are to be "Exhibit A" as to what it looks like to be a Christian. If we don't keep our hands clean, we are giving a wrong impression of Christianity to those around us.

Summing It Up

Sometimes sin can be fun, but it always has consequences. Often, we make a poor decision—and make a lousy trade as a result. Short-term gain for long-term pain.

There are consequences of keeping our hands clean too. Our lives will likely be a whole lot less complicated, for one. Sure, we may miss some fun—but the things we gain by avoiding sin count for eternity.

And sometimes those consequences of keeping our hands clean can be real lifesavers. Psalm 18 was written after David escaped the murderous King Saul. Check out a couple of verses from that psalm.

> The LORD has dealt with me according to my righteousness;
>> according to the cleanness of my hands he has rewarded me. (v. 20)

> The LORD has rewarded me according to my righteousness,
>> according to the cleanness of my hands in his sight. (v. 24)

David was convinced that his efforts to "keep his hands clean" were noticed—and rewarded—by God. I can't think of any better reason to work at keeping our hands clean too.

If we feel we've messed up—and our hands aren't clean—we can confess that to God and to anyone else we may have wronged. God forgives us, cleans us up, and gives us a new start.

> If we confess our sins, he is faithful and just and will forgive us our sins and purify us from all unrighteousness. (1 John 1:9)

Now that's some great truth that we can hang on to, right?

LEGO Lesson

THEME: Building toward the man or woman God wants us to be

THINGS YOU'LL NEED

- ☐ Box of LEGOs. You could get by with a pile of LEGOs, but the visual impact is greater if you can buy a new box of LEGOs. It's the photo on the front that we'll key in to, so try to pick up a box that would be of interest to them. If one of your kids is into *Star Wars*, for example, there are tons of great-looking LEGO sets to choose from. Pick something they'd like to keep and assemble themselves.
- ☐ Optional: if you have a bunch of LEGO pieces around, scoop up a handful of them to use as an additional visual later.

Advance Prep

No advance prep needed. Your big job is to get the LEGO set—and keep it hidden until you're ready to get the kids together for family devotions.

Running the Activity

With this lesson, the LEGOs are more of a visual than an object lesson. *After you're done with the lesson you'll give the LEGO set to the kids to assemble—but not during it.* Since there is no object lesson / activity for this one, you can move right on to teaching the lesson.

Teaching the Lesson

I'm holding a box of LEGOs. One of the things about a LEGO set is that they always have a great-looking picture on the box. But what do you get when you open the box? Bags of pieces and an instruction manual. LEGO sets don't come ready-made. You have to build them . . . one piece at a time.

And this is a great illustration of life. We can have a great picture in our minds of what our lives will be like . . . what *we'll* be like. But that doesn't come ready-made either. Our lives—the people we become—are built one piece at a time.

If we opened this box of LEGOs, we'd find a variety of pieces. Different shapes, sizes, and colors. And there are all sorts of things that build us into the person we become.

- **Experiences.** The things that happen in our lives—good and bad—are like little LEGO blocks. They piece together to form the person we become. God doesn't waste anything. When we go through a tough experience, it becomes part of us. The lessons we learned and the convictions we formed will stay with us. So even bad things in our lives can build us into better people.
- **Choices.** Every day we make tons of choices. We choose to be kind—or not. We choose to obey—or not. We choose to do well at whatever we're doing—or not. We choose to do what is right even when nobody is looking—or not. Every choice—good or bad—is like a LEGO piece added to who we become. Our choices reveal the type of character we are building—and the type of person we'll grow to be.
- **Education.** Certainly, the level of education we get adds to who we become and what we can do.

- **Family.** The family we grow up with adds pieces to our LEGO project. Ideally, these should strengthen who we become.
- **Friends.** The friends we choose can build us up in healthy ways—or tear us down. They can encourage us to build good things into our lives—or they can influence us to compromise and corrupt ourselves.
- **Genetics.** There is a certain element of genetics involved with who we become. For example, our physical features are already blueprinted to a large degree.
- **Dedication to God.** Following God, loving him, trusting him, obeying him—all this and more certainly define us and the person we become. If we go to church and follow God only because that is how we are raised, we will not have many "spiritual LEGO pieces" to add to the person we become. If we choose to follow God—not simply because that's what our family does but because that's where our hearts are—then we add strong, key, defining LEGO pieces to who we become. And this dedication to God isn't just a feeling or a decision. It's action. It's about reading our Bible so that we know him—and know how to live. It's putting what we read into practice. Of all the things that build us into the people we become, our dedication to God is the most important.

> Blessed is the one
>   who does not walk in step with the wicked
> or stand in the way that sinners take
>   or sit in the company of mockers,
> but whose delight is in the law of the Lord,
>   and who meditates on his law day and night.
> That person is like a tree planted by streams of water,
>   which yields its fruit in season
> and whose leaf does not wither—
>   whatever they do prospers. (Ps. 1:1–3)

There are more things, but you get the idea. The person we grow to be is not solely genetics—which is really terrific news. *We have a lot of control over the person we become.*

We said that LEGO sets don't come ready-made, and inside every box there are bags of pieces and an instruction manual. If we don't follow the instructions, likely the end result won't look as good as the picture on the front of the box, right?

- As we apply the whole LEGOs example to life and the picture of the person we want to become, what do you think the LEGOs instruction manual represents?
- Do we, as Christians, have a manual that shows us how to build our lives?
- It is natural for us to look only at the person *we* want to become. But have we considered God? Does he have plans for us? Does he have a picture of the person he wants us to become?

For we are God's handiwork, created in Christ Jesus to do good works, which God prepared in advance for us to do. (Eph. 2:10)

God has plans for us. Things he's created us to do. If we want to become all God designed us to be, it only makes sense that we carefully follow the Bible—God's instruction manual for us—and put into practice what he teaches us to do.

All Scripture is God-breathed and is useful for teaching, rebuking, correcting and training in righteousness, so that the servant of God may be thoroughly equipped for every good work. (2 Tim. 3:16–17)

Summing It Up

If I had a little pile of LEGOs and gave you a few minutes to build whatever you wanted, you'd probably come up with something interesting. But if I gave you a *huge* pile, and you had all day, you'd likely build something phenomenal.

Remember, every experience and every choice is adding to your pile. Your family, the friends you choose—all of these make a difference. And ultimately, following God for real—not just because Mom and Dad do or because we want you to but because *you* want to—will help you become the person God designed you to be. And that is going to be one amazing person—if you do it his way!

A Special Word for Parents

I'd give them the LEGO set after you're done with the teaching time. Save the box—and maybe display it somewhere with a note taped to it saying something like this:

You have a partial picture of the person you want to become . . . and God has the whole picture. May you always follow his Word and make wise choices to become all he designed you to be.

Every time they see that box, they'll have a good reminder of the lesson. And when something bad happens, or they have a tough day, point out the box and talk to them about the LEGO pieces they probably added through that hard experience. Those tough times will help form their character and perspective the way God wants—so they can do all the jobs he has planned for them.

Sack of Potatoes 1

We need to forgive others of the wrongs they do to us

THINGS YOU'LL NEED

☐ Large potato for each of the kids—the kind used for making baked potatoes

☐ Permanent markers (one for each of the kids)

☐ Gallon-size plastic food storage bags

Advance Prep

Other than picking up the above supplies, no advance prep is needed for this one. But there are three things you need to know or be thinking about before you teach this lesson:

1. **There's a second part to this object lesson/activity.** "Sack of Potatoes 2" is the sequel, and you'll want to wait about three weeks or so

before running that one. Why? In today's lesson, we're stressing the need to forgive. In the sequel, we're stressing what happens when we don't forgive. At the end of today's lesson, we'll seal those potatoes in plastic storage bags. After a few weeks, the potatoes will begin to rot. This will help illustrate how failing to forgive actually hurts us.

2. **Examine your heart.** Is there someone you need to forgive—even though they don't deserve it? Is there someone you're holding a grudge against? Ask the Holy Spirit to help change your heart. Forgive them. Then you'll be ready to teach this lesson. Remember Jesus's teaching about getting the beam out of your own eye before you remove the speck from someone else's eye.

3. **Reach back in your memory.** Can you think of examples you may be able to use when teaching the kids this lesson? A time when you were forgiven—but didn't deserve it? Or maybe a time when someone failed to forgive—but should have?

Running the Activity

Gather the kids around the table and pile the sack of potatoes in the center.

- Invite each of the kids to pick a potato and a permanent marker.
- Ask them to write on the potato the names or initials of anyone they are holding a grudge against or anyone they haven't forgiven. They can also use a symbol or code word instead of using a person's name or initials. Let's face it . . . one of your kids may resent someone in the room at this moment.

If they're having a hard time coming up with anyone, that could be a really good thing. Maybe they're doing really well at forgiving—or maybe you need to prime the pump a bit. Here are some ideas for that.

- Can you think of someone who embarrassed you, and you still resent them?
- Can you think of someone who wronged you, and you're still upset with them?

- Can you think of someone who used to be a friend, but they turned against you—and now things are really awkward between you or you feel like enemies?

- Imagine you found a magic lamp. You rub it and the "revenge genie" appears and offers to get even with three people of your choice. Who would you ask him to pay back?

- Can you think of a teacher who was unfair to you or maybe gave you a lower grade than you deserved?

- Can you think of someone who said nasty things about you behind your back—or online—and you still have a hard time with that?

- Do you feel Mom or Dad has let you down in some way, and you just can't get past it?

- Do you feel resentment toward God, maybe because he didn't answer a really important prayer or because of some aspect of your life right now?

Teaching the Lesson

When we've been wronged, sometimes we talk things out with that person and everything is fine again. But many times things don't fully get resolved. That's when we have a choice to make.

1. We can choose to forgive that person—even if they aren't asking for forgiveness. Even if they don't think they did anything wrong. Even if we don't feel they deserve forgiveness.

2. We can choose not to forgive them—and hold on to resentment and anger toward them.

3. We can choose to pay them back and even the score.

The Bible makes it clear that we're to go with option 1.

For if you forgive other people when they sin against you, your heavenly Father will also forgive you. But if you do not forgive others their sins, your Father will not forgive your sins. (Matt. 6:14–15)

Does this even sound fair?

Well, actually, it is fair. God forgives us when we don't deserve it, and he expects us to do the same for others. To do any less than that suggests we may have a pride problem—or that we're not truly grateful for how God forgave us.

Then Peter came to Jesus and asked, "Lord, how many times shall I forgive my brother or sister who sins against me? Up to seven times?"

Jesus answered, "I tell you, not seven times, but seventy-seven times.

"Therefore, the kingdom of heaven is like a king who wanted to settle accounts with his servants. As he began the settlement, a man who owed him ten thousand bags of gold was brought to him. Since he was not able to pay, the master ordered that he and his wife and his children and all that he had be sold to repay the debt.

"At this the servant fell on his knees before him. 'Be patient with me,' he begged, 'and I will pay back everything.' The servant's master took pity on him, canceled the debt and let him go.

"But when that servant went out, he found one of his fellow servants who owed him a hundred silver coins. He grabbed him and began to choke him. 'Pay back what you owe me!' he demanded.

"His fellow servant fell to his knees and begged him, 'Be patient with me, and I will pay it back.'

"But he refused. Instead, he went off and had the man thrown into prison until he could pay the debt. When the other servants saw what had happened, they were outraged and went and told their master everything that had happened.

"Then the master called the servant in. 'You wicked servant,' he said, 'I canceled all that debt of yours because you begged me to. Shouldn't you have had mercy on your fellow servant just as I had on you?' In anger his master handed him over to the jailers to be tortured, until he should pay back all he owed.

"This is how my heavenly Father will treat each of you unless you forgive your brother or sister from your heart." (18:21–35)

Forgiving others can be really tough. Painful. But remember, it will never be as painful as it was for Jesus to forgive us. That act of forgiving us cost Jesus his life.

What about someone who is abusive?

Does forgiving someone mean we keep taking their abuse—or stay silent?

Definitely not. We can forgive someone—which means we truly hold no resentment against them. But we aren't required to keep allowing ourselves to be abused. Sometimes we need to talk to parents or teachers or someone in authority about the situation.

Does forgiving someone mean we must trust the person who wronged us?

Absolutely not. We can forgive someone, but unless God has fully changed their heart, we are not expected to trust them. David forgave Saul for his many attempts to kill him—but David didn't trust Saul not to try again. David was careful to keep his distance from Saul. Forgiveness is something we freely offer, but trust is something that is earned over time.

Summing It Up

Bear with each other and forgive one another if any of you has a grievance against someone. Forgive as the Lord forgave you. (Col. 3:13 NLT)

This verse pretty well sums up this lesson. We need to forgive others—just like Jesus forgives us. We forgive others out of gratitude for what Jesus did for us. What if we just can't seem to forgive? What do we do?

1. *Remember that Jesus was motivated by love.* Maybe the real reason we are having trouble forgiving someone is because we don't have enough love for that person.

2. *Ask the Holy Spirit to give us love for that person.* Love is one of the fruit of the Spirit. In other words, love is one of the things that will grow out of our lives when we surrender our lives to him.

3. *Pray for the person we can't seem to forgive.* It's amazing how that act alone can soften the resentment we have for them.

Now . . . back to the potato. I want to encourage you to forgive each of the people who are represented on your potato.

Let's put each potato in a plastic bag. In a few weeks, we'll revisit this topic and see how you're doing with forgiving others.

A Special Word for Parents

Make sure the seal is locked tight on the storage bags, then stash the potatoes away for a few weeks—until the potatoes are rotting. Then you're ready for "Sack of Potatoes 2." In the meantime, pick other lessons from this book each week to use for family devotions.

Sack of Potatoes 2

THEME: Refusing to forgive others hurts us . . . and our relationship with God

THINGS YOU'LL NEED

☐ The potatoes that you sealed away in plastic bags at the end of the earlier "Sack of Potatoes 1" lesson.

Advance Prep

When you did "Sack of Potatoes 1" (lesson 28) with the kids, you ended by sealing some potatoes in reusable plastic bags. It may take several weeks for those potatoes to start decomposing, so you'll need to wait until that happens. When you see strange growths appearing on the potatoes—or there's brown juice in the plastic bags because the potatoes are rotting—you're ready to do this lesson.

Running the Activity

Get the kids together and hand each of them their potato—still sealed in the plastic bag. Have them observe the changes to the potatoes.

- Are there strange white roots growing out of the "eyes" of the potatoes?
- Do the potatoes look shriveled up in any way?
- Do you see any brown juice from the decomposing potatoes?
- Does anyone want to dare opening the bag and taking a whiff?

Teaching the Lesson

Potatoes, sealed up like this, get pretty weird and nasty over time. And the same thing happens when we fail to forgive someone.

How do some people get "weird" when they fail to forgive others?

Sometimes they become almost obsessed with the person they haven't forgiven. They want to talk about them. Complain about them. And they expect others to do the same. Sometimes friends start avoiding them because they get tired of hearing about the same old things over and over. Like those strange growths coming out of the potatoes, it all gets a little weird.

How do some people get a little nasty when they fail to forgive others?

When we fail to forgive others, generally we'll develop a bitter attitude. We'll shrivel up in some ways. We'll be quicker to criticize, quicker to get angry, quicker to complain, and more likely to think life is unfair. We'll find it harder and harder to forgive—even the small things. Like that rotten juice coming out of the potatoes, our whole attitude begins to stink.

Take a look at these potatoes again. If you choose not to forgive . . .

- You're going to get a little weird and nasty. Count on it.
- You're disobeying God—which isn't at all smart. There are always consequences when we refuse to live by God's commands.

Summing It Up

Imagine that every time you chose not to forgive someone, their name went on a potato and you had to carry it in your backpack. All day. Every day.

- That pack would get heavy—and slow you down.
- That pack would start to stink—and mess up any other stuff you had in there.

When God commands us to forgive others, he isn't doing it just for the sake of the person we forgive. Forgiving others frees us and benefits us in so many ways. Can you pick out some of those benefits as I read these verses?

> And do not grieve the Holy Spirit of God, with whom you were sealed for the day of redemption. Get rid of all bitterness, rage and anger, brawling and slander, along with every form of malice. Be kind and compassionate to one another, forgiving each other, just as in Christ God forgave you. (Eph. 4:30–32)

- When we forgive others, we please the Holy Spirit instead of grieving him.
- When we forgive others, we become kinder and more compassionate . . . just the kind of person others will want to hang around.
- When we forgive others, we're much more emotionally balanced.
- When we forgive others, we're in a position to enjoy God's blessings and avoid his discipline.

As you look at the potatoes, is there anyone you still need to forgive? Is there any way I can help you do that?

If you're ready to forgive the people you noted on these potatoes, let's get these potatoes out of the house—and throw them in the garbage where they belong.

A Special Word for Parents

If you and the kids threw the bags of potatoes out together, you might want to mention how dumb it would be to come back later, rummage through the garbage, and bring the potatoes back into the house and hide them in their bedroom. In reality, they'll be tempted to do that with the whole forgiveness issue. After they've forgiven someone, they need to be careful not to take that forgiveness back—and hold on to resentment again.

Forgiveness is a very important issue. You may want to come back to this lesson occasionally—just as a reminder.

Bogus Bucks

THEME: Avoiding the temptation to be a hypocrite

THINGS YOU'LL NEED

- ☐ Some kind of fake paper money. This could be paper money from a board game (like Monopoly), fake money that you draw on paper and cut into the size of real money, or even actual counterfeit money. (You may be able to get this from a friend who works in a bank or who owns a store or restaurant where they mistakenly took the bogus bill in.)
- ☐ Ideally, real money in the same denomination as the fake one to use as a comparison. So if you have a fake $20 bill, pick up a real $20 bill.

Advance Prep

Your big job is to get your hands on whatever you're going to use for the fake money. If you get "genuine" counterfeit money, you'll want to see exactly what details confirmed the money was bogus.

For example, I have a counterfeit $50 bill. The ink coloring is pretty good. But the watermark proves the money is counterfeit. There should be a watermark of Ulysses S. Grant imbedded in the currency, but instead the watermark depicts Abraham Lincoln. Someone bleached a $5 bill to remove the ink—and printed a fifty in its place.

If you're using board game money, or something you photocopied, the fact that the money isn't genuine currency will be extremely obvious. That will work great.

Running the Activity

Show the kids the bogus currency and the real equivalent at the same time.

- Which one is a counterfeit bill—and which one is genuine?
- How can you tell which is real and which is bogus?

If you have a counterfeit bill, determining which one is real is a little trickier than if you use some kind of play money.

Teaching the Lesson

If we walked into a store with Monopoly money, other play money, or a photocopied bill and tried to buy something . . . likely the clerk would laugh at us.

- Why do people make counterfeit money?
- Do you think some believe that counterfeiting is easier than working to earn the money honestly?
- If we tried to buy something with counterfeit money, what might happen?
- Do you think the clerk or manager might confiscate the money—or call the police?
- What if we manufactured counterfeit money at home and used it in stores? How much trouble might we get into with the police when we got caught?

This is a picture of what often happens to people . . . especially Christians. God wants each of us to build a life of obedience to his Word. He wants us to be true followers of Jesus.

But there will always be the temptation to shortcut that process somehow. Instead of putting the effort into becoming the person they really should be, many people try to counterfeit it. They *pretend* to be more righteous, or holy, or caring, or loving than they really are. They *pretend* to be a growing Christian—but the only thing that's really growing is their nose (Pinocchio reference). They are living a lie. Another term we use for someone like that is *hypocrite*.

In the Bible, we see that hypocrisy was a big problem for some people. Many religious leaders chose to live a counterfeit life instead of truly being dedicated to God.

- When they gave money in the offering, they made a big show of how much they gave. They wanted everyone to see what they gave—and everyone to think they were super-spiritual.
- When they prayed, they liked to do it out in public so people would think they were super-holy.
- They created all kinds of rules about how someone should live if they truly wanted to follow God (implying they were actually following those rules), but they didn't live that way themselves.
- They were concerned about how they looked to people—not about what their hearts were like . . . what they were like on the inside.
- They were big on telling others how to fix their lives—even though their own lives were totally messed up.

Jesus had a lot to say both *to* and *about* hypocrites.

Why do you look at the speck of sawdust in your brother's eye and pay no attention to the plank in your own eye? How can you say to your brother, "Let me take the speck out of your eye," when all the time there is a plank in your own eye? You hypocrite, first take the plank out of your own eye, and then you will see clearly to remove the speck from your brother's eye. (Matt. 7:3–5)

Woe to you, teachers of the law and Pharisees, you hypocrites! You are like white-washed tombs, which look beautiful on the outside but on the inside are full of the bones of the dead and everything unclean. In the same way, on the outside you appear to people as righteous but on the inside you are full of hypocrisy and wickedness. (23:27–28)

Jesus warns over and over not to become hypocrites ourselves.

- Jesus knows the temptation to become a hypocrite is really strong.
- He knows that hypocrites lose out huge. They never become all God intended them to become, and they lose the rewards that would have been theirs if they had followed God honestly and from the heart.

Like trying to use counterfeit money, pretending to be better than you are is going to end badly for you.

Summing It Up

Rather than put all the effort into living a double life and hiding who we truly are, why not dedicate ourselves to being the real deal? Why not invest our effort where there will be a long-term payout?

Manufacturing counterfeit money will land you in jail eventually. And pretending to be a great Christian—but living a lie—will send you to a different type of jail. It will restrict you in this life. It will rob you of some of the joy, freedom, and growth we enjoy as Christians.

Instead, confess areas where you're living a double life. Ask God to help you . . . to change you and teach you to be a true and dedicated follower of Christ. That's where the real rewards are—in the short *and* the long term.

Therefore, rid yourselves of all malice and all deceit, hypocrisy, envy, and slander of every kind. Like newborn babies, crave pure spiritual milk, so that by it you may grow up in your salvation, now that you have tasted that the Lord is good. (1 Pet. 2:1–3)

Bean Bag Bucket

THEME: Aiming at the kind of character we want to develop

THINGS YOU'LL NEED

- ☐ Bucket—either five- or three-gallon size works fine
- ☐ Bean bags (two) or balls that can be tossed into the bucket
- ☐ Blindfold or scarf to use as a blindfold

Advance Prep

Prep is minimal. Bean bags work best simply because balls tend to bounce out of the bucket easier. If you can't get your hands on a pair of bean bags, take a couple of sandwich bags and fill them halfway with uncooked rice, dirt, gravel, or whatever to make your own. After you get the materials above, you're really all set.

Running the Activity

You're going to give one of the kids a chance to toss the bean bags into the bucket. Make this easy for them. You *want* them to make a basket. So have them stand as close as you want to ensure they'll get the bean bags in the bucket.

After they've successfully gotten at least one of the bean bags in the bucket, tell them they're going to do it again—but this time blindfolded.

- Hand them two bean bags.
- Blindfold them—making sure they can't see.
- Turn them around a handful of times to disorient them a bit.

You want them to miss the bucket this time—and here's the secret to making sure they do. While you're turning them, move yourself in the opposite direction at a slower speed so they aren't aware that you're moving at all. Now, when you stop turning them, you should be about 180 degrees off from where they saw you before the blindfold went on. Likely they'll orient their position based on your voice and take aim accordingly. As long as they didn't notice you moving, their aim will be nicely off.

Remove the blindfold—and let them see how far off their aim was.

Teaching the Lesson

The first time you tossed the bean bags, you made a basket easily. The second time was a whole different story.

The key to hitting a target is what? Aiming. Keeping your eyes on the target. And sometimes even practicing. All of these are keys to hitting a target, right?

The same principles apply when it comes to your character . . . the person you'll grow to become. If you want to hit a target, you have to aim. You have to keep your eyes on it. You have to practice hitting that target.

So what type of character do you want? (Read all or some of these examples.)

- Do you want to be a person who is honest—not telling half-truths?
- Do you want to be a person who doesn't complain?

- Do you want to be a person who is kind to others, even people you don't know?
- Do you want to be a brother or sister who is there for siblings and doesn't lash back, even when they treat you badly?
- Do you want to be a person who encourages others?
- Do you want to be a person who is a good influence on others, urging them to do good things and make good decisions?
- Do you want to be a person who is wise?
- Do you want to be a good friend—the type that is there for your friend—even if they misunderstand you or get mad at you?
- Do you want to develop a reputation for having a good work ethic and being a good worker?
- Do you want to be genuinely responsible and dependable? Doing what you say you'll do—and doing it well—without arguing or complaining?
- Do you want to prove yourself to be trustworthy to your parents and others?
- Do you want to honor your parents—because God asks you to—even when they don't seem to understand you?
- Do you want to be one who treats the opposite sex right, in a way that pleases God?
- Do you want to follow God with your whole heart, not halfheartedly?

There are more character issues we could talk about, but I think you get the idea. As I read this list, what were you thinking? I'm hoping that in your heart you were saying "Yes, yes, yes . . . I want to be that person." If that's the case, know right now that I am extremely proud of you.

- Here's the next question. Do you think that those good character qualities will just happen? Will they just appear in your life naturally as you grow up?
- I'm sure you realize that you have to aim at those things. You need to practice those things so they become part of who you are. The big question here? *What are you aiming at?*

You've just heard a list of character qualities—things you'd like in your life. But you're not going to get there without aiming. Without keeping your eyes on those goals. Without practicing.

Will you do that? And remember, you won't be alone. God will help you if you ask him to.

> Therefore, my dear friends, as you have always obeyed—not only in my presence, but now much more in my absence—continue to work out your salvation with fear and trembling, for it is God who works in you to will and to act in order to fulfill his good purpose. Do everything without grumbling or arguing, so that you may become blameless and pure, "children of God without fault in a warped and crooked generation." Then you will shine among them like stars in the sky as you hold firmly to the word of life. (Phil. 2:12–16)

> I thank my God every time I remember you. In all my prayers for all of you, I always pray with joy because of your partnership in the gospel from the first day until now, being confident of this, that he who began a good work in you will carry it on to completion until the day of Christ Jesus. (1:3–6)

> Now may the God of peace, who through the blood of the eternal covenant brought back from the dead our Lord Jesus, that great Shepherd of the sheep, equip you with everything good for doing his will, and may he work in us what is pleasing to him, through Jesus Christ, to whom be glory for ever and ever. Amen. (Heb. 13:20–21)

Summing It Up

As parents, part of your job is to help your kids develop good character. So, with this lesson in mind, realize a key to truly helping them is to help them keep their eyes on that target. How will you do that?

Here are two ideas to consider.

1. Many families have a growth chart on the wall somewhere. It's great to measure our kids' physical growth . . . but how about a "character growth chart" that you make and hang in a prominent place?

   Work with the kids to create a list of character qualities they'd like to see in themselves. Just hanging that list up is a way to keep their eyes on it, don't you think? And maybe you can make little notes on that chart. When you see your kids demonstrating good character, why not note it on their chart? It would be a way to encourage your kids to grow in the right direction.

2. If your kids are old enough, why not start them reading Proverbs—a book that is all about teaching us wisdom and the value of good character? The book of Ruth is another good choice. Look at the character qualities of Boaz and Ruth.

Our culture puts athletes and celebrities in front of our kids all the time. Even though we may not intend to make those people into role models, it's natural for our kids to go in the direction they're looking. So be sure you're frequently showing your kids examples of people who are heroes because of their *character*, not because of how well they play a game or how popular they are.

Give Them a Hand

THEME: **Does God give us more than we can handle? Yes . . . but he doesn't expect us to handle it alone**

THINGS YOU'LL NEED

- ☐ Sturdy chair—the type you'd have at the kitchen table
- ☐ At least four people able to help carry one of the kids sitting in that chair

Advance Prep

Ultimately, you're going to put one of the kids in a chair, then with the help of at least three others, you'll all carry that person in the chair across the room. It would be good to practice this once before doing it with the kids.

Running the Activity

Sit one of the kids in the chair. Since you'll be carrying that person, you may want to choose your smallest/lightest child.

Now, position one of the kids directly behind the chair and give these instructions.

"This chair needs to be carried, with (name of child) on it. He or she needs to be carried all the way across the room. The chair can't be dragged or slid. It must be carried. Do you think (name of child behind the chair) is able to do that?"

None of the kids will think their sibling is strong enough to do that—and of course they're right. Now explain that you never said she or he had to do it *alone*. Suggest that all of you do it together.

Position somebody at each leg of the chair—including yourself and your spouse. If you have two kids to a leg, that's fine too. Now, together with the kids, lift the child in the chair, carry them across the room, and carefully set them down.

If you want to make it even more fun, have a grand, kingly entrance song cued up on your phone and play that while you parade across the room. Epic movie soundtracks are good for that.

Teaching the Lesson

Carrying the chair across the room with someone sitting in it was a pretty impossible job for one person to do alone. But with all of us working together, it wasn't hard at all. In fact, it was kind of fun, wasn't it?

This is often like life. Sometimes there are things we must do that would be very difficult—or even impossible—to do by ourselves. But often we try to do things on our own when God never intended us to do that.

- "God never gives us more than we can handle." Have you ever heard people say that?
- Does anybody know where that's found in the Bible?

The truth? Many people treat that quote like it comes right from the Bible, but that statement is not found in the Bible at all.

And the quote isn't even true. In fact, in the Bible we often see God putting people in situations where they are way over their head.

- **David** . . . facing a giant alone. Or up against jealous King Saul and his army.
- **Job** . . . who lost his kids, his wealth, his health, his friends, and more when Satan put him through the wringer.
- **Moses** . . . facing off against Pharaoh. Or when he was trapped between Pharaoh's army and the Red Sea. Or when he led hundreds of thousands of Israelites across the Red Sea—and through the wilderness for forty years.
- **Gideon** . . . facing a massive enemy army with his puny band of three hundred men.
- **Josheb-Basshebeth** . . . one of David's mighty warriors, who stood up to—and killed—eight *hundred* enemy warriors in one battle.
- **Paul** . . . who survived the "forty lashes minus one" five times. Who was beaten by rods three times, and once was stoned and left for dead. Three times he was shipwrecked—one of those times he spent a whole night and day out in the open sea. He survived cruel prisons, assassination plots, and more.

Don't tell these Bible heroes that "God never gives us more than we can handle." What we often see in the Bible is that God puts people in positions or allows them to face problems that are totally beyond their capability to deal with.

- Why would God do that . . . or allow that?
- Why does God allow even Christians—even those he loves—to go through problems too big for them to handle on their own?

There are probably a number of good answers. Here are a few.

- God allows us to go through hard times or problems too big for us so that we seek him. If we can handle everything life dishes out, we're much more likely to drift from God—and that definitely wouldn't be good for us, right?

- God allows us to go through hard times or problems too big for us so that we experience his rescue. That causes us to grow in our faith and trust—and builds our relationship with God even stronger.
- God allows us to go through hard times or problems too big for us so that we don't become filled with pride—and destroy ourselves in the process. When we realize we can't do something that needs to be done, we get a proper perspective of our own weakness compared to God's strength. That's a good kind of humility.
- God allows us to go through hard times or problems too big for us so that we'll be a good witness for him and tell others how he rescued us. And we'll be able to encourage others going through similar hard times with the truth that God can help them too.

Here are a few verses to remember when you're facing something that is too big for you to handle.

I can do all this through him who gives me strength. (Phil. 4:13)

Keep your lives free from the love of money and be content with what you have, because God has said,

> "Never will I leave you;
> never will I forsake you."

So we say with confidence,

> "The Lord is my helper; I will not be afraid.
> What can mere mortals do to me?" (Heb. 13:5–6)

Summing It Up

Often in life, we'll be in situations or face things too big for us to handle. We should bring it to God. And bring it to other believers. Ask for help. That is another reason God created the church. When we're locked in with a group of believers, one of the things we do is help each other through those tough times.

But getting back to that saying so many people quote . . . "God doesn't give us more than we can handle." Where *does* that come from? Take a look at this verse.

> No temptation has overtaken you except what is common to mankind. And God is faithful; he will not let you be tempted beyond what you can bear. But when you are tempted, he will also provide a way out so that you can endure it. (1 Cor. 10:13)

Often, this is the verse that many get confused about and take out of context. The verse says that God won't allow us to be *tempted* beyond what we are able to bear. Which is really fantastic, don't you think? If we fall to temptation, we can never say we couldn't help ourselves.

But the verse *doesn't* say God won't allow things in our lives that are completely beyond our capability to deal with on our own. And he does that for our good . . . because anything that drives us closer to him is for our eternal benefit.

> And we know that in all things God works for the good of those who love him, who have been called according to his purpose. (Rom. 8:28)

Tug-o-War

THEME: Winning over temptation

THINGS YOU'LL NEED

- [ ] Rope you can use for tug-o-war. The thicker the better, so it doesn't cut into your hands. Ask around . . . you may find someone who will loan you one. Churches often have them buried in an equipment closet somewhere. Can't get a rope? Use a drop cloth (made out of real cloth, not plastic) or an old sheet. You could probably use a garden hose as an option too.

- [ ] People. Ideally, you'd like to have at least six people to help drive the point home. More is better. Can you find eight people, including your kids? Terrific. Neighbors, friends, nephews, nieces. Find others who will join you on this one.

Advance Prep

Lining up people to help with the tug-o-war will be the only real advance work you'll need to do. The fact that you'll have to round up extras will likely keep you from practicing this in advance, but that should work out fine.

Running the Activity

For this lesson to really work, the results of the tug-o-war won't be left to chance. You're going to decide which side wins—in advance—and then you'll make it happen. Here's how you'll do that.

You pick who is going to be on which side. Start by making the sides fairly even, but don't use all your players. Leave at least two players out of the tug-o-war at this point. These reserve players need to have enough strength to change the outcome of the tug-o-war if they work together.

Explain that you'll start the tug-o-war—but that you'll add reinforcements to one side or the other as you see fit.

Once the tug-o-war starts, send your reserve players in to pull for the side you've already chosen to win.

If your reserve players aren't able to bring a swift victory, be ready to join in there and help.

Once your chosen side has won, you'll probably hear some complaints that you weren't fair. That's perfect—and now you're ready to teach the lesson. If you have extra people present, you can wait until they leave to tie the lesson in, or do it while they're there. It's totally up to you.

Teaching the Lesson

Sometimes temptation is seen as a tug-o-war. One part of you wants to do something that you know is wrong. The other part of you resists—knowing you'll get in trouble, or disappoint us, or disappoint God.

That battle in your heart or mind goes back and forth—until finally one side wins. And do you know which side usually wins? *The side you reinforce.*

- What would it look like to reinforce the side of you that wants to do something wrong? How do you reinforce or strengthen the part of you that wants to sin?
- Can you strengthen the side of you that wants to sin—without realizing you're making it stronger? How?

If you think about something that is wrong . . . and you wonder what it would be like to do that wrong thing . . . and you really think it would be fun or exciting to do that wrong thing . . . or you wish or fantasize that there was a way you could do that wrong thing and nobody would know . . . all these and more are ways that you strengthen the side of you that is being tempted to sin. Every time you do one of these things, you are reinforcing the part of you that wants to sin. If you're a Christian, we call that side your "old nature." Thinking and dreaming about that sin is like adding a person to the sin side of the mental tug-o-war that you're having.

Listen to these verses in James.

When tempted, no one should say, "God is tempting me." For God cannot be tempted by evil, nor does he tempt anyone; but each person is tempted when they are dragged away by their own evil desire and enticed. Then, after desire has conceived, it gives birth to sin; and sin, when it is full-grown, gives birth to death. (1:13–15)

It isn't God who tempts us. According to James 1:13–15, we can set *ourselves* up to be tempted. Often, the thing that gets us in trouble is the fact that we've been *thinking* about doing those wrong things. The more we think about the wrong things, the more we want them. And then the verses we just read say that we're "enticed." Often, that's where the devil or his demons come in. We open the door for them, and they give us an opportunity to do something that the Bible says we shouldn't.

In other words, often the devil or his demons will give you the chance to do that wrong thing you've been thinking about doing. And like the tug-o-war in which the side we reinforced just dragged away the other side . . . the same thing happens with sin. Those verses I read describe someone who gets dragged away.

- Does being dragged away sound like a good thing?
- What did the verses say was the result of reinforcing the wrong side—and being dragged away by sin? What does sin give birth to?

The verses talked about "death" being the result of failing to resist temptation. Now, this could be talking about physical death, but we know that people don't usually drop dead when they give in to temptation.

- Besides physical death, what other kinds of death might we experience when we sin?
- Could it be the death of trust, when Mom and Dad—or others—stop trusting you?
- Could it be the death of dreams? Have you ever heard of someone losing a job, or a place on a team, or other things, simply because they did something wrong and they were found out?
- Could it be the death of respect from others . . . or self-respect?

Yes, there are a number of ways you can experience some form of death—and none of them are good.

- Going back to the example of the tug-o-war, if you really want to beat temptation, what are some ways you can reinforce that "good" side?
- What can you do when your mind keeps wanting to go to wrong things?
- What can you do when friends give you opportunities to do wrong things?
- Do you think sometimes you need to run . . . or call Mom or Dad?

Listen to this verse.

Flee from sexual immorality. All other sins a person commits are outside the body, but whoever sins sexually, sins against their own body. (1 Cor. 6:18)

Yes, sometimes we need to run. Sometimes we need to get away from the situation or the people tempting us. This verse talks about the fact that if the temptation is sexual, giving in is going to hurt you in the long run—no matter how fun it may seem or how good it may feel at first.

Summing It Up

Temptation is like a tug-o-war. It's our "old nature" against our "new nature." And the side we reinforce is the side that wins.

If temptation wins, there is always a price. A death of some sort. That's what the Bible says.

How do we reinforce our new nature? Here's a short list of suggestions. Can you add some ideas of your own?

- Check the rating of a movie *before* you watch it or go to see it with friends. There are even organizations that review movies for appropriate content. Focus on the Family's *Plugged In* is a good example (pluggedin.com). Are there elements of the movie that will reinforce the wrong side of the tug-o-war? If so, find a different movie.

- The same idea goes for books. Check the reviews on Amazon or Goodreads before buying a book or checking it out of the library.

- Does your mind wander into places it shouldn't after you go to bed? Try reading some verses from the book of Proverbs just before you hit the lights. Fill your mind with good things.

- Make reading your Bible a daily thing. Not just a little one-page devotional . . . but actually read the Bible. Now, after you've done that, each day decide on at least one thing from the passage that you'll put into practice—starting that very minute. This adds some real muscle to the right side of the tug-o-war.

- Pray. Ask God to give you *new* desires and thoughts . . . the kinds of things he wants you to think and dream about. "Take delight in the LORD, and he will give you the desires of your heart" (Ps. 37:4). Never underestimate the power of the Holy Spirit to change you—when you give him permission to.

- Rethink the friends you hang with. Do they help you reinforce the right side of the tug-o-war? If they're pulling you the wrong way, you'll need to pull away from them.

- Talk to your parents—or a youth leader. Often, they can help encourage you to reinforce the right side of the tug-o-war.

It is my hope that you resist temptation. That you run from it. Don't let your mind and your desires for wrong things drag you away and make you vulnerable when an opportunity pops up.

God always gives us a way out of temptation.

> No temptation has overtaken you except what is common to mankind. And God is faithful; he will not let you be tempted beyond what you can bear. But when you are tempted, he will also provide a way out so that you can endure it. (1 Cor. 10:13)

This verse says God provides a way for you to endure or escape a temptation, but often that way out is very early in the temptation. That's when you need to run.

So the next time you start thinking about how much fun it would be to do something wrong, get your mind on something else. Run. Resist. Be strong.

Someone once described Christians as having two dogs inside them. One wants to do wrong. The other wants to do what is right . . . the things that would please God. They said you can always tell which dog will win. How? The dog that wins is the dog you've been feeding.

It goes back to what you've been thinking about, right? Thinking about the wrong things is feeding and strengthening the wrong dog.

Do you want to win when you're tempted to do wrong things? Good. Feed the right dog.

Weighed Down

THEME: The need for salvation

You'll want to collect various weights that you can attach a rope to. The whole idea is that you'll tie these weights onto one of your kids. Ideally, gather fifty to one hundred pounds of weights. Here are some suggestions.

- ☐ Do you have barbells? Using individual weight plates works great.
- ☐ Hand weights for exercising (dumbbells).
- ☐ How about a boat anchor? Ask to borrow one from a neighbor or someone from church.
- ☐ Know a scuba diver? Weight belts work great.
- ☐ Even a heavy box or bin that you can tie a rope around will work.

You'll also need:

- ☐ Rope to tie to each weight. Figure about three to five feet of rope per weight.
- ☐ Chair (kitchen or folding type)

Advance Prep

Each of the weights needs a rope attached *before* you do the devotion with the kids so you can quickly tie them around the wrists, ankles, or waist of your volunteer.

Running the Activity

Sit one of the kids in the chair and explain that you're going to add some weights to them. With the weights resting on the floor or on their lap, take the free ends of the ropes and tie them to their wrists, ankles, and maybe around their waist. Be careful not to tie anything too tight. You don't want to cut off their circulation. And you don't want to tie any knots that will be hard to undo. You'll need to take the weights off them later as part of the lesson.

Once you've got all the weights tied to the one in the chair, you're ready to move on.

Teaching the Lesson

There are many weights attached to (name of child). Let's imagine these weights aren't simply tied on but are permanently attached.

- Can they live with all this weight on them? Could they survive?
- It wouldn't always be very fun, but they would live, right? It might be easier for them to sit in a wheelchair so they wouldn't have to lug all this stuff around . . . but they could go through life with the extra weight. Would you agree?
- What is one thing they absolutely *couldn't* do with all this weight on them?

The one thing they couldn't do with all this weight is *swim*. Imagine them trying to get across a large lake—or the ocean. Impossible.

This is a picture of life. The weight represents sin in our lives. Everybody sins, and we cannot shed the weight of our sin by ourselves.

For all have sinned and fall short of the glory of God. (Rom. 3:23)

Now, we can live with sin—just like we could live with these weights tied on us. Our sin may slow us down, but we can survive.

But sin is rebellion against God. The presence of sin in our lives makes us enemies of God. And there is a penalty that must be paid for sin. The penalty for sin is death.

Once you were alienated from God and were enemies in your minds because of your evil behavior. (Col. 1:21)

For the wages of sin is death. (Rom. 6:23)

Let's imagine that heaven and God are on the other side of a great body of water. Our sin separates us from God. We certainly can't get to heaven on our own—not with that weight of sin. Our sin would drag us down to certain death.

But God loves us too much to leave us in that state of carrying the weight of our sin . . . and being his enemies . . . and being impossibly separated from him and heaven.

But God demonstrates his own love for us in this: While we were still sinners, Christ died for us. (5:8)

- God offers us a free gift.
- He offers us peace with himself.
- He offers us forgiveness for every one of our sins.
- He offers to free us from the weight of that sin . . . because Jesus, God's Son, paid the price for our sin by dying on the cross. And Jesus was raised to life again.

God offers all of this to us as a free gift—even though our sin makes us his enemies. But he wants us to surrender completely and unconditionally.

- Salvation isn't about making a peace treaty with God.
- It isn't about negotiating some kind of agreement.
- It is throwing ourselves at his mercy. Knowing we have nothing to offer him. No way to buy our salvation. No way to bargain for it. We simply surrender to him.

Some people refer to this as making a "commitment to Christ," but possibly the best picture of us coming to God for the forgiveness of sins is *surrender*.

When we truly surrender and give our lives to Christ, we are no longer God's enemies . . . and the weight of our sin is gone. One way to show our gratitude and appreciation for all he's done for us is to avoid sin—and with his help, strive to live in a way that is pleasing to him.

Summing It Up

Most people don't like the idea of surrendering. On December 7, 1941, the Japanese attacked the US Navy base at Pearl Harbor, and twenty-five hundred people were killed and one thousand were wounded. Eighteen US ships and nearly three hundred planes were destroyed or damaged.

It was an act of war . . . and the United States and Japan became enemies. The United States was determined that a price would have to be paid for that attack. Years of battles followed—and by 1945 the United States had developed the atomic bomb. In light of that horrendous weapon, and the fact that most of Japan's navy and air force had been destroyed, the United States demanded Japan's unconditional surrender in the Potsdam Declaration.

Japan refused to surrender, and the atomic bomb was dropped on the city of Hiroshima with devastating results. An estimated eighty thousand people were killed.

Japan still refused to surrender, and another atomic bomb was dropped on the city of Nagasaki.

Finally, Japan surrendered—unconditionally. And the United States began to help rebuild that war-torn nation.

But still, some Japanese soldiers didn't want to surrender.

It took twenty-nine years after the war was over for at least two Japanese soldiers to finally surrender. Hiroo Onoda surrendered in the Philippines in March 1974, and Teruo Nakamura surrendered in Indonesia in December 1974.

All those years they thought surrender would be a bad thing . . . but they'd missed so much. The United States had helped rebuild Japan, and the nation was a strong, vibrant world power again.

We were once enemies of God. We carried a weight of sin that would end only in death—and eternity in hell. But God loved us too much to leave us in that hopeless situation, and he made a way for us to be saved. But he expects our complete and unconditional surrender.

If you haven't truly surrendered to him, why wait any longer? God wants to free you from your weight of sin—and build you into something really, really good.

Good Fear

THEME: Fear of the Lord

THINGS YOU'LL NEED

- ☐ A 4 x 4 post, about 8 feet long—or anything similar that can be used as a balance beam
- ☐ Two chairs, sturdy plastic bins, or anything similar to support the balance beam no more than a couple of feet off the ground
- ☐ Scarf or something similar to use as a blindfold
- ☐ Optional: couch cushions or pillows on the floor around the beam

Advance Prep

Support the balance beam so that it remains stable. You'll want to test it to be sure. When you actually do this lesson, one of your kids will walk across it—with your supervision, of course. You'll need to make sure the beam is secured so it can't tip and cause anyone to fall.

KEEP IT SAFE

We don't want any injuries here. It would be wise to keep the area around the balance beam clear. You don't want anything there that might hurt your child should they fall off the beam. You may even want to arrange couch cushions and pillows on the floor around the beam.

Also, you don't want your child to fall. So you must stay close enough to spot them—and catch them if they lose their balance. You may even walk on the floor alongside them, holding their hand to steady them while your spouse—or someone else responsible—does the same on the other side, especially during the blindfolded portion of the activity.

Running the Activity

Have the balance beam all set and secure. Invite one of the kids to walk the beam. If your kids are too young for this, you or your spouse could walk the beam and it would still be a great and effective visual.

Let your child have a few turns on the balance beam. And once they're feeling pretty secure, let them do it one more time while you have someone else in the family record a video of them on your phone.

Now, you'll have them walk the balance beam again—but with the blindfold on. You'll be right next to them the whole way to prevent a fall. Be sure your helper records the blindfolded walk too.

Here are the things we're hoping to see.

- That your volunteer walks much slower when they're blindfolded.
- That your volunteer is much more cautious when they're blindfolded.

Perfect. You're ready to teach the lesson. Have your child take off the blindfold and step carefully off the beam.

Teaching the Lesson

When our volunteer walked the balance beam with the blindfold, it was a whole lot scarier for them, wasn't it? How could you tell they were a bit more scared with the blindfold on? Let's look at the video clip.

- Did they walk slower?
- Did they crouch over more—with their hands out to their sides for balance?
- Did they look less confident?
- Were they more open to getting help—or wanting to make sure their spotter was there to catch them?

Sometimes fear is a really bad thing. It keeps us paralyzed. It keeps us from moving forward and doing what we should do.

And sometimes fear is a good thing. It helps keep us safe. Just like with the balance beam here. It was obviously more dangerous when they couldn't see, and we saw how that little bit of fear made them more cautious—and kept them safe as a result.

The Bible talks over and over about the "fear of the Lord"—and how it's a good thing.

> Let all the earth fear the Lord;
>> let all the people of the world revere him. (Ps. 33:8)

> The angel of the Lord encamps around those who fear him,
>> and he delivers them. (34:7)

> The fear of the Lord is the beginning of wisdom. (111:10)

> Blessed are all who fear the Lord,
>> who walk in obedience to him. (128:1)

> Humility is the fear of the Lord;
>> its wages are riches and honor and life. (Prov. 22:4)

> The fear of the Lord leads to life;
>> then one rests content, untouched by trouble. (19:23)

> The fear of the LORD is the beginning of knowledge,
> but fools despise wisdom and instruction. (1:7)

"Fearing the Lord" . . . what is that all about?

- Fearing the Lord is about having a healthy respect for God.
- It is about honoring him enough to obey him.
- It is a sense of humility, knowing God is God—and we are not.
- It is acknowledging that since God is God, we should be careful to do what God says.
- It is knowing that God sees all we do, hears all we say, and knows all we think.
- It is realizing that God loves us, definitely. But God is also just, meaning he must deal with sin.

So a healthy fear of the Lord can be a good thing. It keeps us in line. And that may be just the thing that keeps us safe—and out of traps that could hurt us.

> The fear of the LORD is a fountain of life,
> turning a person from the snares of death. (14:27 NLT)

The "fear of the Lord" isn't stressed only in the Old Testament. It's a very real part of the New Testament as well. In Acts 5 we read the story of Ananias and Sapphira. This husband and wife sold a piece of property and claimed they were giving the entire amount of the sale to the church. But they really kept some for themselves. Now, there was nothing wrong with them keeping the money—but they lied and said they gave it all to appear more spiritual.

God struck them both dead. And twice in that chapter God talks about something that swept through the church as a result.

And great fear seized all who heard what had happened. (Acts 5:5)

Great fear seized the whole church and all who heard about these events. (v. 11)

A great fear spread through the church. *The fear of the Lord.*

- A fresh sense of respect and awe.
- A belief that nobody could fool God—and it was senseless to try to live a hypocritical double life.

People often talk about the early church in Acts, and how wonderful it must have been to be with believers who sacrificed for each other the way they did. People read in Acts how the church exploded with growth as more and more people were saved. But many miss an important element . . . something that made that church so great.

The fear of the Lord.

Take a look at how God is careful to point out that the fear of the Lord was essential to the church. In two sentences, God sums up what the early church was all about.

> Then the church throughout Judea, Galilee and Samaria enjoyed a time of peace and was strengthened. Living in the fear of the Lord and encouraged by the Holy Spirit, it increased in numbers. (9:31)

The fear of the Lord was an essential element to the church in Acts—and it is still needed today. The fear of the Lord is something that is often missing in today's church. It isn't even on our radar. As a result, Christians make compromises in the way they live. Too often they fail to put the principles from the Word into practice.

Today we like to think of God as only a God of love and grace and forgiveness. But he is also to be respected with a healthy fear. Jesus made that pretty clear in the Gospel of Luke.

> I tell you, my friends, do not be afraid of those who kill the body and after that can do no more. But I will show you whom you should fear: Fear him who, after your body has been killed, has authority to throw you into hell. Yes, I tell you, fear him. (12:4–5)

The more you read your Bible, the more you'll see the importance of the fear of the Lord. Not a cowering fear, but a fear that if we go our own way instead of being careful to put the Word into practice . . .

- God may have to deal with that sin.
- We may hurt ourselves by stepping into painful traps.

- We may distance ourselves from God . . . the very One who wants to help us every step of the way.

Summing It Up

One of the things that made the blindfolded balance beam walk scary was that they couldn't see where they were going—or what was happening next. The Word says that we don't know what tomorrow will bring. Only God knows that.

> Now listen, you who say, "Today or tomorrow we will go to this or that city, spend a year there, carry on business and make money." Why, you do not even know what will happen tomorrow. What is your life? You are a mist that appears for a little while and then vanishes. Instead, you ought to say, "If it is the Lord's will, we will live and do this or that." (James 4:13–15)

In a way, we go through life with a blindfold on. We can make plans, but we don't know what tomorrow will bring. And we have enemies, the devil and his demons, who want to trap us and get us to fall into sin.

But God sees. He knows the future. He sees the traps. And he wants to help us walk through life.

In light of all this . . .

- Wouldn't it make sense to walk carefully—to be thinking about how we are living? To make sure we are staying on God's path?
- Wouldn't it make sense to slow down in life enough to be sure we're staying close to God? Holding tightly to his hand? Asking him to guide us?
- Wouldn't it make sense to be sure we aren't wandering from him—afraid that if we do we'll get hurt or we'll be missing something?
- Wouldn't it make sense to be obedient to God so that he wouldn't have the need to discipline us?

That's a lot of what the fear of the Lord is about. No wonder Proverbs says "The fear of the LORD is the beginning of wisdom" (9:10)!

Messy but Valuable

THEME: You still have value—even when your life is a mess

THINGS YOU'LL NEED

- ☐ $20 bill. You can do the lesson with a $10 bill instead . . . but the bigger denomination may make the point of the lesson even more clear.
- ☐ Plate, disposable or not . . . either works
- ☐ Ketchup. A squeeze bottle works great.

Advance Prep

Other than getting your supplies, no advance prep is needed for this one.

Running the Activity

Hand one of the kids the $20 bill. Explain that the $20 bill is yours—and you're going to keep it when the lesson is over.

- Ask them to crumple the bill into a ball.
- Ask them to toss the crumpled bill onto the floor or ground.
- Ask them to stomp on the crumpled bill.
- Hold out the plate and ask them to put the crumpled bill on the plate.
- Hand them the ketchup and ask them to cover the bill with ketchup.

Perfect. Their job is done now. Hold the plate for the kids to see—and you're ready to teach this important lesson.

Teaching the Lesson

Wow . . . what a mess. Now that my money has been crumpled and trampled and covered with ketchup . . . do you think I still want this $20 bill?

Yes, I *definitely* want this money. Why do you think I'm going to keep it instead of throwing it into the garbage?

- The money is just a mess, that's all. I can clean it up, right?
- The money still has value.
- In fact, the money is *just as valuable* as it ever was.

Sometimes we can be a little like this $20 bill. As we've raised you over the years, we've tried to show you how valuable you are—and how much you're loved. But sometimes life has a way of making any of us feel our value is gone.

- Maybe you don't feel that you're the most handsome or prettiest. But that's just surface stuff.
- Maybe you're getting bullied, or you don't have friends. Or you don't feel like you're very popular. Your sense of value goes way down. But your value is never tied to how many friends you have or how others treat you.

Your real value is about who you are *inside*. Your character. And that is something that continues to grow and develop.

- Maybe you've really messed up somehow—and you know it. You've made a mistake. Gotten involved in sin. You've failed somehow or let someone down. It's easy to see your value going down too. But just like the ketchup on the $20 bill . . . messes can be cleaned up over time.

No matter how you feel about yourself—or how others make you feel—you still have all the value that you ever had. Nobody can take that away from you. You're unique. You bring something special to everyone you're around—things only you can bring. That's how God made you.

And that brings us to the deeper truth of this lesson. God loves you so much that he died for you.

But God demonstrates his own love for us in this: While we were still sinners, Christ died for us. (Rom. 5:8)

"While we were still sinners." Are you catching that? While we were in the most messed-up position a person could be in. We were ruined by sin. Doomed. And yet God loved us enough to die for us—and make us his children.

Never forget this truth: he doesn't love us less if we've made a mess somehow.

Summing It Up

I'm keeping this $20 bill. It's a mess, but I can clean it up. It isn't worth a penny less than $20 to me. It's the same way with each of us . . . with our value.

If we've made some kind of mess of our lives, or made some big mistake, we can go to God. He can clean us up and make everything right.

If we confess our sins, he is faithful and just and will forgive us our sins and purify us from all unrighteousness. (1 John 1:9)

If we feel we lack value based on how others treat us or look at us, or how we view ourselves, remember . . . God made us this way for a purpose. His purpose. And that means we have great value.

Thinking on these truths should give you some hope and a proper perspective. You're special. *Really* special. Jesus died for you . . . that means you've got real value.

So if you're feeling less than valuable right now, there are four things you need to do or remember.

1. **Talk to me.** Tell me about it—and let me help you see the situation from a different perspective.
2. **Talk to God about it.** Realize God is absolutely famous for turning tough situations into wonderful stories. For making good things come from bad. Things beyond our imagination. God has a reputation for turning people who question their value into people clearly used by him for something really, really special.
3. **Trust God.** It will get better. You have great value. Beyond what you can possibly comprehend.
4. **Know that God loves you.** Don't ever doubt his love for you. Listen to these verses and see just how much God loves you.

And we know that in all things God works for the good of those who love him, who have been called according to his purpose. For those God foreknew he also predestined to be conformed to the image of his Son, that he might be the firstborn among many brothers and sisters. And those he predestined, he also called; those he called, he also justified; those he justified, he also glorified.

What, then, shall we say in response to these things? If God is for us, who can be against us? He who did not spare his own Son, but gave him up for us all—how will he not also, along with him, graciously give us all things? Who will bring any charge against those whom God has chosen? It is God who justifies. Who then is the one who condemns? No one. Christ Jesus who died—more than that, who was raised to life—is at the right hand of God and is also interceding for us. Who shall separate us from the love of Christ? Shall trouble or hardship or persecution or famine or nakedness or danger or sword? As it is written:

> "For your sake we face death all day long;
>   we are considered as sheep to be slaughtered."

No, in all these things we are more than conquerors through him who loved us. For I am convinced that neither death nor life, neither angels nor demons, neither the present nor the future, nor any powers, neither height nor depth, nor anything else in all creation, will be able to separate us from the love of God that is in Christ Jesus our Lord. (Rom. 8:28–39)

Storm Survivor

THINGS YOU'LL NEED

- ☐ Bowling ball—twelve pounds or *heavier*
- ☐ Bowling ball—eight pounds or *lighter*
- ☐ Container to drop bowling balls into (a clear container is nice, but you can also use a trash can)
- ☐ Bucket to fill container with water

Advance Prep

The trickiest thing is to find the bowling balls at the right weights. Here are two suggestions. Both worked for me.

- Put a message out on social media, asking to borrow the bowling balls you need.
- Go to a bowling alley to see if you can borrow bowling balls. I had good success with this. When they hear you'll use them for a type of science experiment to teach your kids life principles, likely they'll be willing to help. When I mentioned this, they went in the back room, found some balls that had been there for eons, and let me keep them.

Now, fill your container nearly to the top with water and test the bowling balls. The heavier one should sink, but the eight-pounder should float. Perfect. Before the kids get involved, remove and dry the bowling balls.

Running the Activity

I've got two bowling balls here. They're both regulation size, about 27 inches around.

Put a bowling ball in water and what happens? (Drop in heavier one.) It sinks.
Let's try another one. (Drop in lighter bowling ball.) This one floats!
Why does one bowling ball sink and the other float?

- One is heavier—or more dense—than the other bowling ball.
- The denser bowling ball is heavier than the same volume of water, so it sinks.
- The less-dense bowling ball is lighter than the same volume of water, so it floats.

The two bowling balls may look pretty equal sitting on the table, but when we put them in water, *the difference is obvious*.

Teaching the Lesson

The word *dense* is sometimes used to describe someone who does something really dumb or foolish. They are "thickheaded" and not using their brain.

Jesus told a parable about two builders. One was wise—and the other was *dense*. He was foolish.

> Therefore everyone who hears these words of mine and puts them into practice is like a wise man who built his house on the rock. The rain came down, the streams rose, and the winds blew and beat against that house; yet it did not fall, because it had its foundation on the rock. But everyone who hears these words of mine and does not put them into practice is like a foolish man who built his house on sand. The rain came down, the streams rose, and the winds blew and beat against that house, and it fell with a great crash. (Matt. 7:24–27)

- Both heard the Word. But only *one* obeyed consistently.
- Both heard the Word. But only *one* put it into practice.
- Both heard the Word. But there were two very different responses to it.
- One was wise, and he survived the high waters . . . the storms of life.
- One was foolish . . . he was dense, and he went down.

Many hear the Bible. Maybe at church, through a sermon, in a family setting like you're in right now, or by reading it themselves.

But it isn't enough to just *hear* what the Bible says. We must put it into *practice*.

In other words, we must do what the Bible says. That's the only way to stay on track with the good plans God has for us. That's the only way that we'll survive the storms and the temptations of life.

So when we read a verse that says we need to honor our mom and dad . . .

- What would be an example of how we could put that into practice?
- What would be an example of how we would not put that into practice?
- What would it look like to honor our parents in the way we talk to them—or about them?

And when we read a verse that says we need to do everything without complaining or arguing . . .

- What would it look like if we actually put that verse into practice?
- Arguing and complaining . . . would that include how we talk to our brothers and sisters?
- Is whining a form of complaining?

When we read a verse that says we should not lie . . .

- What about telling a half-truth?
- Are there ever times that we can be telling a lie without saying a word?

And we could go on and talk about how we're to love others, forgive others, and be kind to others. It is not enough to hear the Word . . . we must put it into practice.

Summing It Up

Some people think the Bible is restrictive. But it is all about protecting us. Often, the times we don't stay on track—the times we don't put the Word into practice—are the times we make mistakes. Those are the times we do something that makes a mess, gets us in trouble, or brings us regrets.

The Bible puts it this way in Proverbs:

> The highway of the upright avoids evil;
>> those who guard their ways preserve their lives. (16:17)

I want to encourage you to stay on track, to put the Word into practice in all you do and say. It's for your own good.

- And if we're *wise*, that's exactly what we'll do.
- But if we're *dense*, we'll make excuses. Maybe we feel we're an exception to God's rules. Or maybe we're waiting for someone else to obey God first . . . then we'll obey too. This would not be wise.

But we need to remember: storms are coming. They always do. And if we're living dense, the high waters will bury us.

Do not merely listen to the word, and so deceive yourselves. Do what it says. Anyone who listens to the word but does not do what it says is like someone who looks at his face in a mirror and, after looking at himself, goes away and immediately forgets what he looks like. But whoever looks intently into the perfect law that gives freedom, and continues in it—not forgetting what they have heard, but doing it—they will be blessed in what they do. (James 1:22–25)

Mug Cake

THEME: Self-esteem and trusting God to make something good of our lives

THINGS YOU'LL NEED

- ☐ ¼ cup all-purpose flour
- ☐ ¼ cup granulated sugar
- ☐ 2 tablespoons unsweetened cocoa powder
- ☐ ⅛ teaspoon baking soda
- ☐ ⅛ teaspoon salt
- ☐ 3 tablespoons milk
- ☐ 2 tablespoons canola or vegetable oil
- ☐ 1 tablespoon water
- ☐ ¼ teaspoon vanilla extract
- ☐ 2 small mixing bowls
- ☐ Large microwave-safe mug to bake the cake
- ☐ Access to a microwave oven
- ☐ Can of ready-made frosting

If you prefer to eliminate the sugar, substitute 1½ tablespoons plain unsweetened applesauce (and mix it in with the wet ingredients during the activity). If you need to eliminate the dairy, use an additional 3 tablespoons plus 1 teaspoon of water instead of the milk.

Advance Prep

Prepare a mug cake of your own when the kids aren't around so you see exactly how to make this. Here are the basic instructions.

1. Mix flour, sugar, cocoa powder, baking soda, and salt in a microwave-safe mug; stir in milk, oil, water, and vanilla extract.
2. Cook in microwave until cake is just done in the middle, about one minute and forty-five seconds. Let rest for a couple minutes.

Running the Activity

- Have all the dry ingredients (flour, sugar, cocoa powder, baking soda, and salt) stirred together in a small mixing bowl.
- Have all the wet ingredients (milk, oil, water, and vanilla extract) in a second mixing bowl.
- Now get the kids together for the lesson.

I have a variety of edible things in these two bowls.

Let's say one bowl represents things about you. Your personality, intelligence, and abilities. And the other bowl represents things that happen to you in life. Good things and bad things.

Now, since all of this is edible, I'd like to have one of you take a small teaspoonful from one of the bowls here.

How do you like the taste of it? How often would you like me to serve you something like this?

The fact is, it really doesn't taste very good, right?

- But let's mix them all together in this mug.
- And let's put this mug in the microwave.
- Now, let's watch as we microwave it for a minute and forty-five seconds.

Would anybody like to guess what we're making?
Would any of you like a bite of this once it's done baking?

Teaching the Lesson

The mug cake tastes a whole lot better than some of the ingredients did before we mixed them together and baked them, right?

That's the way it is with life too. There are all kinds of aspects of our lives that we may not be all that excited about.

- We may wish we had more abilities, better looks, more smarts.
- We love the good things that happen to us in life—but we probably feel that we can live without the bad stuff.

But remember, the cake needs every one of these ingredients—most of which don't taste good by themselves. Our lives are no different. Our lives are made up of things that "taste" good and things that "taste" bad to us. And just like the cake, we need all those elements in our lives to make us into the person God wants us to be. God uses all those elements—good and bad—and can make something really good out of them.

And we know that in all things God works for the good of those who love him, who have been called according to his purpose. (Rom. 8:28)

What would happen if we had the power to stop any hard or bad thing from happening to us? Is it possible that we would never become all God designed us to be? You can be sure of that.

Summing It Up

What if, after mixing all the ingredients together in a mug, we never put the mug inside the microwave? What would we get? A mug of goopy stuff, right? The heat—the baking—solidifies the cake batter into something more solid and tasty.

And it's the same way with us. There are times in life when we go through an oven of sorts.

- We face the heat of some kind of hurt, maybe from a friend or because we don't have one.
- We face the heat of some kind of change—in ourselves or our family—and we don't like it.
- We face the heat of a missed opportunity, an embarrassing moment, or messing up in some way. We'd do just about anything to change that, but we can't.

Just like the microwave oven turned the goop into a cake, the hard times in life often produce something unexpected and good in us. Sometimes the heat is needed to solidify us into someone who is so much better—or better off—than we would have been otherwise.

- When you feel dissatisfied with your abilities, your intelligence, all the things that make you who you are . . . give it to God.
- When you feel discouraged about some hard thing you're going through or mistake that you've made . . . give it to God.

He produces great things that you'd never expect. Things that you'll really, really like.

I've got a can of frosting here to finish our mug cake off just right. And this is a reminder as well. When we give ourselves to God . . . when we believe he uses the good things that happen and the bad, our abilities and inabilities—he makes something good and solid. And, as a result, our trust in him grows—and that's just like the frosting on the cake. The frosting makes the whole thing so much better—and worth it. And when our trust in God grows, it makes all of life that much better. We're more free from worry and fear and insecurities—because our trust in him drives those away.

In Judges 6, we read about Gideon. He was a nobody in a family of nobodies. Yet God used him to lead a small band of men to overpower a massive enemy army. What a great reminder for us. Trust God to make great things of your life— even when nothing may seem that big or great to you right now.

A bunch of ingredients, none of which tasted good, led to a nice little surprise. They were mixed together and put in the heat—transforming the goopy mess into a great little cake. God does the same things with our lives when we offer ourselves to him in love and obedience.

The Most Dangerous
Cake Recipe

THEME: **Resisting temptation**

THINGS YOU'LL NEED

If you did the mug cake in lesson 38, you'll find you're going to use the same recipe here to illustrate a completely different point.

- ☐ ¼ cup all-purpose flour
- ☐ ¼ cup granulated sugar
- ☐ 2 tablespoons unsweetened cocoa powder
- ☐ ⅛ teaspoon baking soda
- ☐ ⅛ teaspoon salt
- ☐ 3 tablespoons milk
- ☐ 2 tablespoons canola or vegetable oil
- ☐ 1 tablespoon water

- ☐ ¼ teaspoon vanilla extract
- ☐ 2 small mixing bowls
- ☐ Large microwave-safe mug to bake the cake
- ☐ Access to a microwave oven
- ☐ Can of ready-made frosting
- ☐ Safety glasses—one pair for everyone who will be present

There's nothing dangerous with this activity, but the safety glasses set things up perfectly for talking about the *dangers* of temptation. If you haven't invested in safety glasses yet—do it. You can purchase them for just a few dollars at the hardware store, and you'll use them for a number of other lessons in this book.

Advance Prep

If you haven't made a mug cake before, prepare one of your own when the kids aren't around so you know exactly how to make this. And be sure to eat the evidence. Basically, it's like you're making one giant cupcake. Here are the instructions.

1. Mix flour, sugar, cocoa powder, baking soda, and salt in a microwave-safe mug; stir in milk, oil, water, and vanilla extract.
2. Cook in microwave until cake is just done in the middle, about one minute and forty-five seconds. Let rest for a couple minutes.
3. Slather a generous amount of frosting on top.

Running the Activity

- Have the batter all mixed and ready to go in a mug as the kids gather.
- Place the mug in the microwave.
- Set the timer for one minute and forty-five seconds.
- Make sure everyone puts on safety glasses—including yourself.
- Turn the microwave on so the cake is baking while you talk.

Okay, kids, I've set the microwave for one minute and forty-five seconds. And we're about to make the most *dangerous* cake recipe I've ever seen.

- Can anybody guess why this cake is so dangerous?
- Do you think it's because I've put something nasty in the ingredients?
- Do you think that the combination of ingredients makes this toxic somehow?
- Do you think this "batter" is really some kind of plastic explosive?

When the timer rings, take the mug out of the microwave—but be careful, it's hot. Now open the can of frosting and spread it on nice and thick.

Actually, there's nothing toxic in the cake and no explosives in the batter. What makes this recipe so dangerous? *The fact that I can make it so quickly.* In under two minutes I can make a personal cake. How is that dangerous?

Because it's quick, I could easily bake a personal mug cake every day. How good would that be for my health? Not good at all, right? But the fact that it's so easy and so quick makes it *tempting* for me to bake a mug cake more often than is good for me.

Teaching the Lesson

We live in a world where we're surrounded by temptation.

- We can be tempted to skip reading our Bible—and absorb social media instead.
- We can be tempted to seek friends who are popular—but not always the best influence.
- We can be tempted to get lazy with living out our faith—especially at home. Often, we can use our words and behavior to treat parents and siblings in ways the Bible clearly tells us we shouldn't.
- We can be tempted to do *good* things—and avoid the *best* things.
- We can be tempted to spend our time on things that won't count for eternity.

- We can be tempted to buy the lies the enemy wants us to believe. Like God doesn't care about us, God doesn't have a plan for us, our lives will never amount to anything, and the list goes on.
- And with the technology in our phones, we can be tempted to access things that would be wrong for us to view as Christians.

Let's sink in a bit on the whole issue of phones, because they can be such a huge source of temptation.

What makes them especially dangerous is the fact that we can give in to temptation so easily. For example, accessing something wrong on our phones can happen a whole lot faster than it takes to make the most dangerous cake in the world. We don't need two minutes. It takes only seconds.

When a fisherman casts a lure into the water, he intends to catch fish—not feed them. Lures have hooks. The fish that thinks a lure is lunch *becomes* lunch. And that's the way it is with temptation. The devil and his demons tempt us to bite on their lures, and they have plenty of them. If we chance a bite, the enemy has us on his hook—and we're not going to like how he reels us in.

Our phones can be like lures—and they've definitely got hooks. Our phones can tempt us in a number of ways.

- **Accessing pornography.**
- **Getting involved in conversations that are unwholesome** or that don't encourage or build others up.
- **Wasting the gift of time that God gives us.** Look around. You'll see people with their noses glued to their phones—even when they're out with others. We can spend so much time messing with our phones that we don't relate to others or complete the plans God has for us. We don't notice others in need—or help them—because we're wrapped up with our phones. So many times when we feel we "have a minute" to spare, we go to our phones. But we're generally there a lot longer than a minute. The things our phones give us access to tempt us . . . *lure* us into spending more time there than we'd planned.
- **Keeping our minds constantly occupied so we don't think about God or hear his voice.** It's not to say that music, video games, texting,

movies, or the millions of apps are inherently wrong or sinful for us—but if they keep us from God, his Word, and the work he wants us to do, they certainly can be.

These things are toxic for us. And they're especially dangerous because they're quick and easy.

You might have friends who bite on the very lures they should be avoiding. You may notice that those friends or acquaintances don't seem to suffer any ill effects. They are enjoying life. They're popular. It almost seems like there are no hooks for them—or that they somehow beat the consequences.

Don't be fooled by appearances. Sometimes the devil and his demons use other kids as bait. They've bit on the lure of temptation, but the enemy doesn't reel them in right away. He lets them appear happy. They seem to be popular.

It's not that these kids don't have hooks in them. You just don't see them yet. That's how the enemy lures others to take the same bait. Remember, there is always a consequence for giving in to temptation. The enemy will make that person pay—and the price is always more than giving in to the temptation was worth.

Now that I know how to make a mug cake, what keeps me from making one for myself every day? Or twice a day? That's going to take a little self-control.

And it is similar for us as Christians when it comes to avoiding things that aren't the best for us. In fact, Christians have a handful of ways to help beat temptation.

1. **A strong desire to be faithful to God.** That's a heart thing, right? That strong desire will help us beat temptation.

2. **Self-control.** Desiring to be faithful to God, we push ourselves to say no to things that are wrong.

3. **Holy Spirit control.** Knowing that it's hard to do the right things at times, we can pray—asking God to change our hearts through his Holy Spirit. The Holy Spirit can weaken our desires for things that are wrong and strengthen our desire to be faithful to God.

4. **Accountability.** We are honest with someone who will help us stick to our convictions to do the right things and to choose wisely. Often, parents are the ones God has provided in our lives to help us do this.

I'm going to zero in on the whole sexual aspect of temptation for a moment. The enemy will tempt you to look at things you shouldn't. Maybe a friend of yours will want to show you something they pulled up on their phone. Be careful. Avoid it. Turn and run if you need to. These things will hurt you in the long run so much more than you can possibly realize now. God's Word emphasizes that. Here are a couple of things he says in the Bible—and there are plenty more.

> Flee from sexual immorality. All other sins a person commits are outside the body, but whoever sins sexually, sins against their own body. Do you not know that your bodies are temples of the Holy Spirit, who is in you, whom you have received from God? You are not your own; you were bought at a price. Therefore honor God with your bodies. (1 Cor. 6:18–20)

Summing It Up

A mug cake can be pretty tempting—it is so quick and easy. But it wouldn't be good for us if we gave in to the temptation to make one every day, right? How much more important is it to be careful not to fall into the temptations around us—especially since they are so quick and easy?

Here's an important verse to remember.

> You who are young, be happy while you are young,
>> and let your heart give you joy in the days of your youth.
> Follow the ways of your heart
>> and whatever your eyes see,
> but know that for all these things
>> God will bring you into judgment. (Eccles. 11:9)

Yes, we want you to enjoy your life, but remember that you must answer to God for how you choose to live. And it all starts with the heart. Like David, we can pray that God will help change our hearts so we're not drawn to things that are wrong.

> Do not let my heart be drawn to what is evil
>> so that I take part in wicked deeds
> along with those who are evildoers;
>> do not let me eat their delicacies. (Ps. 141:4)

The verse ends with a line about not eating of their "delicacies." It goes back to the fishing example. The enemy always makes the bait look good—but there are always hooks.

Do you want to beat temptation—and the inevitable consequences of sin?

- Make sure that your desire to be faithful to God is strong.
- Exercise self-control.
- Give the Holy Spirit permission to change you.
- Open up to Mom or Dad so we can help you be accountable.

Make this your prayer:

> Search me, God, and know my heart;
>   test me and know my anxious thoughts.
> See if there is any offensive way in me,
>   and lead me in the way everlasting. (139:23–24)

Pick Your Poison

THEME: Dangers of compromising, letting the world seep in

THINGS YOU'LL NEED

☐ Paper and pen for each person (or phone camera)
☐ Access to a grocery store

Advance Prep

Take a run to the grocery store and go down the aisle that stocks household cleaning solutions. Take some time to look at the ingredients portion of the labels. All you're looking for are products that have the "harmful or fatal if swallowed" warning. At the very least, you should find plenty of labels warning of the danger of ingesting the cleaner—with instructions to immediately call the doctor or a poison center hotline.

Another place you could check is the aisle where they carry traps and poison for mice. The poison generally will have exactly the type of warning label you need.

Once you've identified products with these kinds of warnings, you'll know just where to lead the kids and won't be fumbling around reading labels while they're with you.

Running the Activity

Once you're at the grocery store with the kids, take them to the aisle(s) you're going to focus on and give them each paper and a pen. Or, if the kids have a phone, they can use that to snap pictures instead.

- Give them fifteen minutes to record as many product names as they can that contain some kind of warning like "poison," "harmful or fatal if swallowed," or "if ingested call doctor immediately."
- Also have them note a couple of variations of exactly what the warning said—and the steps to be taken if the product was actually swallowed.

Now, you'll have their notes or pictures to go from when you teach the lesson after the fifteen minutes are up—but you won't actually do that at the grocery store. Teach them at home or, better yet, take them to a fast-food restaurant.

Why a fast-food restaurant? When your kids get in the house, they tend to scatter. You'll have to round them up to teach the lesson. At a fast-food restaurant, kids generally are expecting to sit together as a family as soon as they get their food or snack.

Teaching the Lesson

Let's look at your notes and pictures.

- How many different products did you find that were dangerous or fatal if someone swallowed them?
- Does anyone have a favorite "warning" to share?

We were in a grocery store that was loaded with all kinds of food. Much of it was healthy food. Fruit. Vegetables. Milk. Yogurt. Bread. But in the middle of all of this food that we need to stay alive, there were tons of products that could kill us, right?

This reminds me a little of life.

We're surrounded by many things that are good for us. Family. Friends. Church. Education. But even though there are all those good things, there are also things that are bad for us. Things that would be toxic for us as Christians. Can anybody think of an example?

- Certain friendships can be toxic.
- There are things we could read or watch that would work like poison on us.

In a way, we're a bit like a grocery store. As Christians, we should be stocked with many good things. Our entire lives are to be "Exhibit A" as to what being a Christian is all about. We're to be an example to others of how a Christian should live.

> Don't let anyone look down on you because you are young, but set an example for the believers in speech, in conduct, in love, in faith and in purity. (1 Tim. 4:12)

But sometimes there's some poison in us—right in there with all that good stuff. Sometimes we let our "grocery store" of good things get stocked with some bad things. Like what?

- How about our attitudes? Couldn't bad attitudes work like poison on us?
- How could pride hurt us?
- How could an unforgiving heart be toxic for us?
- How could a selfish "me first" attitude be harmful or fatal if swallowed by us?

We know all these things are wrong for us as Christians. They're compromises. What are some other compromises we can make as Christians? What are some other areas in which we can let the ways of the world seep into our lives?

- What about disobedience?
- What about areas of dishonesty or breaking trust?
- What about the way we talk to brothers, sisters, parents, or others?
- How can being unkind or inconsiderate be toxic?
- How can worry be toxic for us?

In the Bible, we read many stories of people who compromised. Instead of doing what was right, they hid the wrong things or discounted the danger. We can read story after story in which that compromise worked like poison and hurt them. Adam. Eve. Cain. Abraham. Lot. Jacob. Moses. Aaron. Achan. Samson. David. And the list goes on.

Now, we understand that the grocery store needs to stock all kinds of things for its customers—including things that are toxic. But as Christians, I hope we'll work to keep the poison of compromise out of our lives.

King David had his moments when he messed up—but he had a heart that didn't want to compromise. You can sense that in his prayer here.

> Search me, God, and know my heart;
>   test me and know my anxious thoughts.
> See if there is any offensive way in me,
>   and lead me in the way everlasting. (Ps. 139:23–24)

We can do that too. Ask God to show us our compromises—and ask him to help us change them.

Summing It Up

Take a look at the pictures of those labels again, or the notes you wrote. If someone swallowed one of those toxic substances, how long should they wait before they take action?

They need to act immediately, right? They're to call the doctor or the poison hotline. They're to either drink liquid—or not—depending on what the label said.

What does that tell us about how fast we're to react when we realize we've got something toxic in us? When we see we're compromising somehow—and allowing something in our lives that is wrong or dangerous?

- Would you do that? Would you bring it to God—like David did in his prayer?
- Would you take some action to make a change?
- Is there someone you need to say you're sorry to?

Talk to me about it too. I'd love to help.

Balance Beam

THEME: **THEME:** Forgetting the past and focusing on the future

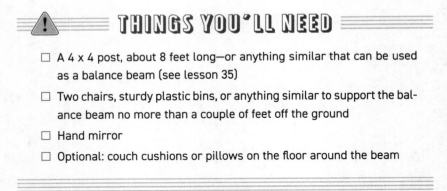

THINGS YOU'LL NEED

- ☐ A 4 x 4 post, about 8 feet long—or anything similar that can be used as a balance beam (see lesson 35)
- ☐ Two chairs, sturdy plastic bins, or anything similar to support the balance beam no more than a couple of feet off the ground
- ☐ Hand mirror
- ☐ Optional: couch cushions or pillows on the floor around the beam

Advance Prep

When you practice this prior to meeting with the kids, I'd suggest you don't even use the balance beam. Walk a straight line on the floor. But instead of looking ahead, hold the hand mirror out in front of you and focus on looking at what is *behind* you while you walk *forward*. Do your best to block out your peripheral vision. The more intent you are on solely looking in the mirror, the better. Clearly, your progress will be slowed a bit by looking *backward* when you're trying to move *forward*.

After you've practiced this a couple of times, you may want to try the beam—but don't go overboard here. You don't have a spotter, so I wouldn't elevate the 4 x 4 at all. Just lay it on the floor.

Running the Activity

Let the kids have a turn walking the balance beam. Depending on their age, you may want to hold their hand while they do this to steady them and keep them from falling. At the very least, spot them. Walk alongside them—staying close—so you can catch them or steady them.

Now have the kids walk the beam again—but while holding a hand mirror. Be sure they're fully focused on the mirror and what is behind them instead of what's in front of them.

Teaching the Lesson

Walking the balance beam is doable while you're looking forward. But when we added the mirror and asked you to focus on what was behind you, that made it a lot trickier, right?

This is a picture of what can happen to us at times in life. Sometimes we get so focused on something that happened in the past and think about it so much that it is hard for us to move forward.

In the Bible, we see a number of examples of others who had that issue.

- **Moses.** In Exodus 3–4, God wanted Moses to go to Egypt and tell Pharaoh to free the Israelites. Moses kept looking at the mistakes of his past. Based on his past, he saw himself as a failure. He was afraid nobody would listen to him. On top of that, he had a speech problem—or at least wasn't confident speaking up in front of others. The past, the past, the past. Moses couldn't move forward. He didn't see how his future could be any different from the failures of his past.

- **Joshua.** After a battle had gone terribly wrong, Joshua got on his face before God—and stayed there all day. He was grieved at the loss of life the Israelites had experienced. He kept looking at the defeat. He even began wishing they'd never come to this land. He was majorly focused on what was behind him—not the task in front of him. In Joshua 7:10, God told Joshua to get up. He asked why Joshua was staying on his face before God. The reason Joshua's men had been defeated should have been obvious. Someone had sinned—and that had kept God from blessing the army with victory. Joshua needed to stop grieving about what was past and start moving forward to find out who had sinned and punish them for it.

- **Gideon.** In Judges 6, the Israelites were overrun by bands of raiders who ruined their crops and killed their livestock. The Israelites hid in the mountains and in caves. God sent an angel to give Gideon a message. God had chosen Gideon to free his people from this great oppression. But Gideon wasn't at all excited about this. He recounted their history to the angel, telling how God no longer helped them. And he talked about himself—that he was a nobody. Gideon had his eyes in the rearview mirror and missed the fact that God wanted to do something new—to free the Israelites— and he was going to use Gideon to do it. God wanted to turn Gideon the *worrier* into Gideon the *warrior*.

There are so many examples of people in the Bible who couldn't get past their past. People who were focused on the things that had happened to them historically—instead of looking ahead to see what God might want to do for their future.

How have you seen this total focus on the past in your life or in the life of someone else?

- Maybe someone can't get over how they messed up on something. A failure. A sin.
- Maybe someone can't get over the fact that they missed an opportunity.
- Maybe someone can't get over the fact that they didn't measure up . . . didn't make the cut for a team or something else.

There are all kinds of mistakes and failures and missed chances that we can focus on or beat ourselves up about. But if we keep looking at the past, likely we'll miss what God has planned for us for the future.

How do we get past our past?

If it involves something we did wrong, we need to confess to God. And likely we'll have to ask forgiveness from someone we may have hurt or offended too. Realize God forgives—completely.

> If we confess our sins, he is faithful and just and will forgive us our sins and purify us from all unrighteousness. (1 John 1:9)

> > For as high as the heavens are above the earth,
> >   so great is his love for those who fear him;
> > as far as the east is from the west,
> >   so far has he removed our transgressions from us. (Ps. 103:11–12)

Sometimes we have to move on from our past.

- **Maybe we keep looking at some past failure.** We need to get over it. Change our perspective. See it as part of our life education. Something that developed our character.

- **Maybe we liked a phase of our past a whole lot more than we like our situation now.** If we keep longing for the *good old days*, we'll miss what God has for us now—and for the future. So we should thank God for the good past—and trust him for the future. He has prepared some things he wants us to do (Eph. 2:10).

- **Maybe there is a part of our past that we're ashamed of.** Or we were taken advantage of or abused somehow. If so, we need to talk to someone about that. Parents? Our pastor? Maybe get some good Christian counseling.

Stop and look at your situation. Is there something from your past that you're focusing on too much? Is there something from your past that is keeping you from moving ahead with the life and plans God has for you? Ask God to help you with this. And seek godly counsel from parents or others.

Summing It Up

The apostle Paul was keenly aware of the danger of getting stuck in the past. And in his past, he definitely had some horrible things that he deeply regretted. Paul realized that focusing on his past could discourage him or slow him down from doing what he needed to do in the present.

Here's how he moved forward.

> But one thing I do: Forgetting what is behind and straining toward what is ahead, I press on toward the goal to win the prize for which God has called me heavenward in Christ Jesus. (Phil. 3:13–14)

Let's follow his example. Unless God is preparing you to be a historian, it's time to stop looking at things in the past.

- Put the past behind you.
- Look forward.
- Put effort into whatever God has for you . . . put your energy there.
- Press on—like you're in a race heading for the finish line.
- Strive to accomplish the purposes God has for you—and to receive the rewards he gives when you do.

In other words, set your sights on living the way God wants you to live—and do what he's planned for you to do. Remember that God has prepared great things for those who are faithful to him.

It is important to remember our history a bit. To learn from our mistakes so we don't repeat them. But when we focus on the past too much, we simply aren't living in a balanced way. Living too much in the past just isn't healthy—and eventually it will trip us up. And looking backward too much definitely will keep us from doing what God has planned for us.

Wrong Destination

THEME: Genuine repentance and turning an area of your
life around

THINGS YOU'LL NEED

Cash to buy ice cream or a snack for the kids

Advance Prep

Pick a place where you can take the kids for ice cream or a snack—someplace
the kids will really, really like. You need to have the destination fixed in your
mind before you start this with the kids so you can map out your route to get
there. You'll want to drive close enough to the place that the kids will see it—
but you'll actually drive right past your destination. Have a spot in mind a mile
or so beyond the destination where you can safely turn around and head back.

Here's what you'd like to happen. Since the kids know where you're headed,
likely one of them will notice—and tell you—that you've passed your destination.
The plan is that you'll pretend to be unconvinced at first, then turn around and

go back to the destination after you've driven a mile or so past it. This will open up a talk about what repentance is all about: changing your direction once you realize you've made a mistake.

Running the Activity

For the sake of simplicity, I'm going to refer to the place you've chosen to take the kids as the DQ. Announce to the kids that for family devotions today, you're taking them to the DQ for the treat of their choice.

You're going to drive right by the DQ. If your kids are old enough and notice you aren't stopping, likely they'll say something. If not, set it up for your spouse to point out the fact that you've passed the DQ.

When one of the kids or your spouse tells you that you've passed the DQ, don't even glance in the direction of the place. Just assure everyone, "I know where I'm going. I know how to get to the DQ."

Drive a mile or two—long enough to show you'll never hit the DQ in the direction you're going. Finally, pull over and admit you've passed the DQ.

"Hey . . . I think I must have passed the DQ."

You may get a lot of, "I told you we were going the wrong way" comments. That's great.

Now mention that you've got three options . . . and ask for their input.

1. Forget about getting ice cream and go home.

2. Keep driving the wrong way to see if eventually you'll find another DQ.

3. Turn around and head in the right direction of the DQ you passed.

Likely the kids will suggest you simply turn around and head back to the DQ, which is exactly what you'll do. Once you're there, get everybody their treat and find a table. You've got everything set up perfectly!

Teaching the Lesson

- How many of you knew I was going in the wrong direction?
- At first, I didn't listen when you told me I was making a mistake, right?

- When I finally did admit I was going the wrong way, what is the first thing I did?

I stopped, right? And then I had to make a decision. I could forget about going to the DQ, or find a new spot, or turn around and head back to where I should have gone the first time.

This is like life. Sometimes we take a wrong turn. God is pretty clear about how we should live—but there are times we mess up. We go the wrong way. We end up someplace we weren't supposed to be.

When we're headed the wrong way in life—in our actions, behavior, attitudes, or the things we say—*the first thing we need to do is stop*. When I realized I was driving in the wrong direction, I finally stopped.

- What if that's all I did? What if I only stopped?
- No, stopping wasn't enough. If I was to get to the DQ, what else did I need to do?

I needed to turn around. Go back. Head for that original destination. And it's the same with life. When we realize we're headed someplace other than where God would want us to go—we need to stop. Immediately.

But we need to do more than simply stop. *We need to turn around.* We need to change our direction so we're heading toward being the person God wants us to be.

Does anybody know the term for that—when somebody realizes they're wrong and then makes a real change? We call that *repentance*.

When Jesus met with a tax collector named Zacchaeus in Luke 19:1–10, it didn't take Zacchaeus long to know he'd been heading in the wrong direction. He had cheated people. After meeting Jesus, the man wanted to *stop* doing the wrong things. And he decided to *change direction*. He was so serious about this change that he committed to giving half of what he owned to the poor and to paying back everyone he'd cheated four times the money he'd taken from them. *That's* repentance.

In the book of Acts in the New Testament, we meet Saul, a rising star among religious leaders of his day. Saul had dedicated himself to seeking out Christians and punishing them for their faith in Jesus. But when he fully realized who Jesus was—he immediately *stopped* chasing down Christians. He actually became a Christian and stopped hurting followers of Christ. He *changed direction* and did everything he could to help other people become Christians. *That's* repentance.

Now the big question comes back to each of us: Is there an area of your life where you're going in the wrong direction?

- The way you're treating your brother, sister, or others?
- The way you're talking?
- The way you're getting angry so easily?
- The things you're letting yourself think about?
- The way you make excuses not to pray?
- The way you tend to ignore reading your Bible?
- The way you don't make a solid effort to put into practice what the Bible says?

The first thing you need to do is admit what you're doing is wrong and stop—just like I did when I finally realized I was never going to hit the DQ the direction I was going.

Stopping is a good start, but it is only the beginning. Now you need to change directions—you need to *repent*—and head toward the destination of being the person God wants you to be. How can you do that?

Summing It Up

Remember . . . repenting isn't saying "I'm sorry" but not making a real change. Think about when I stopped the car, realizing I'd passed the DQ. What if I'd told you all how sorry I was, then started up the car and kept going in the wrong direction? How crazy would that have been, right? You would have thought I really wasn't so sorry after all. We have to be careful in real life not to do the same. True repentance is more than admitting we were wrong. It is about changing direction.

And remember one more thing: if you don't turn around, you don't get the rewards.

When I finally admitted I was wrong and stopped—and repented by turning around—we got a nice little treat at the DQ. With true repenting, there are always rewards. The rewards aren't always ice cream. What are some other ways God might reward us if we repent of the wrong we're doing?

What if I had kept driving, even after knowing I had passed the DQ? What if I'd waited and waited and waited before stopping? I'd have had a much longer way to drive to get back to the DQ, right? It's the same with repenting. If we're doing wrong—and we know it—we shouldn't wait to stop and turn around. We'll get to the rewards a lot more quickly that way!

Spudzooka

THEME: Anger—its effects, its roots, and how to defuse it

 === **THINGS YOU'LL NEED** ===

Borrow or build a potato gun. Ask around . . . you'd be surprised how many guys have one of these squirreled away in a basement or garage. They'd love to dust if off and show you how it works.

If building your own, do a quick Google or YouTube search for *potato gun*, *potato cannon*, *potato launcher*, or *spudzooka*. You'll find plenty of plans—and step-by-step building videos. Pick one that's within your comfort level. Some get pretty elaborate, but a basic one will work just fine.

- ☐ Schedule 40 PVC pipe, PVC connecters, and PVC cement, all generally found in the hardware store
- ☐ An igniter—something I get at hardware stores or places where camping supplies are sold. This little gizmo gives off a spark to fire the spudzooka.
- ☐ A drill to mount the igniter and some type of saw capable of cutting PVC. You'll also need a good flat file to sharpen the muzzle opening of your spudzooka. You'll see how to do all this when watching the online building instructions.

Regardless of whether you borrow or make your own spudzooka, you'll need a few more things.

- [ ] Potatoes. Big ones . . . the type you use for baking. The potatoes must be bigger than the inside diameter of the spudzooka muzzle.
- [ ] Hairspray—aerosol type. You don't need expensive stuff. Cheap brands work great.
- [ ] Ramrod. For pushing the potato down the PVC barrel. You can use a five-foot dowel rod—or a broom handle works fine.
- [ ] Safety glasses or goggles for everyone present

Advance Prep

If you're going to make the spudzooka, consider doing it as a family project. It will build anticipation for the devotional. Allow plenty of time to build this—projects always take longer than you think, right? And the PVC cement needs a twenty-four-hour cure time to fully harden. Check the label to be sure.

You'll find there are great videos that give step-by-step instructions for building and shooting your spudzooka. You'll need this—so take the time to watch how it's done.

Definitely set aside some time to practice shooting the finished spudzooka before the devotional time with the kids. Be sure to wear your safety glasses!

1. Select a potato that is bigger than the inside diameter of the PVC barrel.
2. Force it down into the opening of the PVC muzzle. This is why you sharpened the end of the PVC muzzle with the file when you built the spudzooka. The sharp PVC edges should slice right through that potato, making a potato "round" or "pellet" the exact inside diameter of the muzzle. Don't slide the potato all the way down the muzzle yet.
3. Unscrew the cap for the combustion chamber. Spray hairspray inside—maybe for a six-second count—and quickly screw the cap back in place. Try to lose as little of the hairspray aerosol fumes as possible.

4. Using the ramrod, quickly slide the potato the rest of the way down the muzzle until the spud hits the combustion chamber. This compresses the combustible aerosol hairspray gases.

5. Brace the spudzooka against your hip—and be sure everyone present is wearing safety glasses.

6. Aim carefully. Be sure to keep your aim low when you fire—unless you're out in a field or shooting over a body of water. The potatoes fly farther than you might expect.

7. Hold the spudzooka tight—and hit the igniter.

You'll hear a whoosh—and that potato is going for a ride. Congratulations! You'll want to "test" the spudzooka more than once.

- **Round one—go for distance.** Shoot that potato out into a large, clear area.
- **Round two—aim at something hard, solid, and close.** A rock, stone wall, or large tree works great. A practice session for this is smart, because you'll be doing this on devotion day with the kids. Position yourself close enough to the target so that you don't miss, but keep yourself a safe distance away—knowing the potato shrapnel will fly back at you.

Running the Activity

Note: based on how your test-firing of the spudzooka went, you'll want to determine just how much you'll let the kids be involved when it comes to shooting the potato cannon. With younger kids, I generally hold the spudzooka and let one of them trigger it with the igniter.

Run through the loading and shooting steps you did in your advance prep to fire the spudzooka. You may want to shoot the cannon once for each of the kids present.

Be sure to take one more shot afterward to aim at a nearby tree or hard, flat surface (like a wall or rock) so the kids see the potato explode. It would be great if someone captured a slo-mo video on their phone.

KEEP IT SAFE

1. **Be sure everyone present is wearing safety glasses or goggles—all the time.**

2. **Be sure you aim carefully—and use proper gun-handling procedures when using the spudzooka.** For example, you'll want to be sure the muzzle is always pointed at the ground—and not at any of the kids. Never aim the spudzooka at anything that you don't intend to shoot. Never point the spudzooka at another person—even as a joke.

3. **Definitely explain that the spudzooka is something they're not to shoot on their own.** Remind them that you must always be present. And the good thing is that whenever they want you to pull it out again, it will be a chance to remind them about the lesson.

Teaching the Lesson

- Which did you like better? Shooting the potato for distance—or watching it turn into hash browns against that tree (or rock, wall, whatever you aimed at)?

- How many of you would like to shoot more potatoes and let them splatter like that?

- Watching the potato explode was definitely fun. But there's another type of explosion—or rather a way *people* explode—that is not fun or funny at all. Can anybody guess what I'm talking about?

Exploding in anger is no fun for the person who is getting hit with it—and it isn't so great for the person who loses their temper either.

- What types of things make you angry?

- What do you do when you get angry? How do you react?

- Do you ever say something or do something when you're angry that you regret later?
- How might we hurt *others* by what we say or do when we're angry?
- How might we hurt *ourselves* by what we say or do when we're angry?

That's the way it is with anger. Very often it's extremely destructive. The Bible has a lot to say about anger. Here are a few samples.

> My dear brothers and sisters, take note of this: Everyone should be quick to listen, slow to speak and slow to become angry, because human anger does not produce the righteousness that God desires. (James 1:19–20)

Very often our anger will get us into trouble. And not just our anger, but others' as well. If we hang around with people who tend to be hotheads, we're going to get burned. The Bible warns us to steer clear of friends who get angry easily. Like that potato exploding, those who get angry easily make messes—and the people close to them will pick up some shrapnel.

And the Bible warns us to avoid hot-tempered, easily angered friends for another reason. Being a hothead can be contagious.

> Do not make friends with a hot-tempered person,
> do not associate with one easily angered,
> or you may learn their ways
> and get yourself ensnared. (Prov. 22:24–25)

Is it always wrong to be angry?

Can you think of any examples when it would not be a sin to get angry? Sometimes we can have "righteous anger."

- When we hear about sin, the bad things people do—or do to each other.
- When we hear about injustice—when somebody does something wrong and gets away with it.
- When we mess up ourselves—doing something wrong even when we know better.

Sometimes it isn't wrong to get angry about things like this, but the Bible warns us to be very careful with what we do with that anger.

> "In your anger do not sin": Do not let the sun go down while you are still angry, and do not give the devil a foothold. (Eph. 4:26–27)

- Even if we get angry for a *good* reason, we must be careful not to do or say something sinful.
- And we must deal with that anger right away. Burying our anger is really, really dangerous. The Bible says we're to take care of it—pronto.
- If we make excuses . . . if we sin for a "really good reason," or if we let that anger simmer inside us without dealing with it . . . we are in dangerous territory. By doing that we are giving the devil a toehold in our lives. Somebody once said that if we give the devil a toehold, soon he'll get a foothold—and then a stronghold in our lives. Not good.

What can we do to end the anger we have?

- One of the fruit of the Holy Spirit is self-control. We should ask the Holy Spirit to give us the self-control we need to curb our anger.
- And we can also ask God to change our hearts so that we don't get so angry at others.
- We can read the Word . . . see what it says about being angry or hot-tempered. It will help us want to fight anger even more.

What should we do if someone is angry with us?

One thing we can do when someone is angry with us is avoid making it worse. In fact, the Bible says that when we talk nicely and kindly to someone who is angry with us, often they'll calm down.

> A gentle answer turns away wrath,
> but a harsh word stirs up anger. (Prov. 15:1)

You might think, *Isn't it kind of wimpy to be all nice and sweet when someone is yelling at me?*

There isn't anything weak or cowardly about it at all. The Bible says that a person who can be patient or who shows self-control like that is mightier or better off than a warrior who conquers a city.

> Better a patient person than a warrior,
>> one with self-control than one who takes a city. (16:32)

Summing It Up

We live in a world where people are more angry and less patient. Anger fuels road rage and school shootings and plenty of other hurtful things along the way. Anger is often rooted in pride. Proud people see themselves as the most important person in the room. And pride is easily offended. Proud people expect others to recognize their importance—and when that doesn't happen, they get mad. *How dare they do that to me? I deserve better than that.*

As Christians, destructive, hurtful anger shouldn't be part of our lives. That's what these verses talk about. And if we're really mindful of how God forgave us—and loves us—likely we won't have nearly the problem with anger that we might have otherwise. Our gratitude to God should melt away pride. This is how God wants us to live and treat others.

> Do not let any unwholesome talk come out of your mouths, but only what is helpful for building others up according to their needs, that it may benefit those who listen. And do not grieve the Holy Spirit of God, with whom you were sealed for the day of redemption. Get rid of all bitterness, rage and anger, brawling and slander, along with every form of malice. Be kind and compassionate to one another, forgiving each other, just as in Christ God forgave you. (Eph. 4:29–32)

Dead and Buried

THINGS YOU'LL NEED

Note: this is one devotional that you won't do in the winter, unless you live in a warm climate. A little heat is important to make this work.

☐ Ground beef—one pound is plenty (option: you could substitute the beef with some roadkill . . . a small animal you find freshly dead on the side of the road)

☐ Gallon-size plastic food storage bag

☐ Shovel

Advance Prep

This lesson is going to be a little different because you'll teach it in two parts. The second part you'll do as a little follow-up—a week after talking to the kids about forgiveness.

Pick up the ground beef or the roadkill ahead of the devotion—and you're all set. You'll also want to pick a spot where you'll bury the meat as you finish the lesson with the kids. Be sure to mark the spot where the meat is buried—you'll be going back there after a week.

If it's the ground beef, you'll put it in the resealable plastic bag and allow as much air into the bag as you can before sealing and burying it. That will help it rot faster—which is what you'll want. If you're burying roadkill, I wouldn't worry about putting it in plastic first. Totally your call.

Running the Activity

Have the meat out on the table for the kids to see. If you have roadkill—as in a dead animal—let's be sure it's an outdoor table.

You won't actually bury the meat yet. For now, jump right ahead to teaching the lesson—because you're going to bury the ground beef or roadkill after you're done.

Teaching the Lesson

Today I want us to think about forgiveness. Can anybody here recite the Lord's Prayer?

This, then, is how you should pray:

"Our Father in heaven,
hallowed be your name,
your kingdom come,
your will be done,
    on earth as it is in heaven.
Give us today our daily bread.
And forgive us our debts,
    as we also have forgiven our debtors.
And lead us not into temptation,
    but deliver us from the evil one." (Matt. 6:9–13)

In the Lord's Prayer, we're asking God to forgive us in the same way that we forgive others. Can you imagine if God actually *answered* that prayer?

That would mean that if we don't forgive someone—but hold a grudge instead—we're praying that God will do that to us too. Is that what we want?

How thoroughly does God forgive us? How complete is his forgiveness? Let's look at Psalm 103 to see just how forgiving God can be.

> The Lord is compassionate and gracious,
>> slow to anger, abounding in love.
> He will not always accuse,
>> nor will he harbor his anger forever;
> he does not treat us as our sins deserve
>> or repay us according to our iniquities.
> For as high as the heavens are above the earth,
>> so great is his love for those who fear him;
> as far as the east is from the west,
>> so far has he removed our transgressions from us. (vv. 8–12)

God removes the sin from us—as far as the east is from the west. You can't get farther than that.

God wants us to forgive others just like he forgives. In fact, if we don't forgive others—like a sibling or parents or others—what did Jesus, recorded in this passage below, say about how God will forgive *us*?

> For if you forgive other people when they sin against you, your heavenly Father will also forgive you. But if you do not forgive others their sins, your Father will not forgive your sins. (Matt. 6:14–15)

That's a scary thought, right?

I've got some meat here. Let's say that it represents some sin committed against us.

- Maybe someone said something hurtful to us.
- Maybe they were rude to us.
- Maybe we felt cheated in some way.
- Maybe they treated us unfairly, or any number of things.

Whatever that sin against us is—this ground beef represents the sin they committed against us. If the person who wronged us asks for forgiveness, we're to forgive them—just like God forgives us. And when God forgives, he buries our sin in the deepest sea.

> You will again have compassion on us;
>> you will tread our sins underfoot
>> and hurl all our iniquities into the depths of the sea. (Mic. 7:19)

So we're going to take this meat outside, grab a shovel, and bury it. But before we do, let me ask you a few questions.

- **Sometimes, when somebody asks you to forgive them, they also ask you not to tell anybody what they did. Is keeping their secret part of true forgiving?** Actually, sometimes—even though you forgive—you still have to tell someone, right?

- **What if a friend committed murder—and asked you not to tell?** This is an extreme example, but it helps us think this through. Do you have an obligation to tell? Yes; that is what Scripture teaches. To keep your mouth shut is a way of being a false witness.

- **What if someone did something to you that was inappropriate?** Maybe something sexual, in the way they talked to you or touched you? You absolutely must tell an authority figure. Sin can be forgiven—but there are always consequences to sin. If they are asking you to keep their "secret," realize they are trying to manipulate you into helping them avoid consequences. That is abuse. Covering for someone like that—even family—is wrong, and often very dangerous.

- **Does forgiving someone mean that you must trust them and act like nothing ever happened?** Absolutely not. When trust has been broken, you can forgive that person, but it will take a long time before that person might be trusted again—if ever.

- **Do you have any other questions about forgiving?** It is really important that you understand this.

- **Is there a situation in your life in which somebody has asked you to forgive them—and has also asked you to keep that wrong**

thing that they did a secret—and you might need to talk to us about that?

So if there was some sort of crime committed, or abuse, we should realize that we can forgive someone but we also need to talk to someone in authority—not just keep this thing a secret.

But most of the time, when someone has offended us, or said something mean, or whatever, and asked for forgiveness, we don't have to tell anybody about what they did wrong. When we truly forgive . . . it's like we *bury* the sin.

- We don't hold it against the person.
- We don't bring it up again. When it's forgiven, it's over.

So let's grab a shovel and bury this beef, okay?

Summing It Up

A week or so after burying that meat, take the kids back to the burial spot. Hand them a shovel and ask them to dig it up.

By this time the stuff should be rotting. Ask them to take a whiff of it.

Okay, so this meat really stinks, right? We should have left it buried . . . would you agree with that?

And that is one more reminder I want to give you about forgiveness. When we truly forgive someone . . .

- We don't hold the sin against them.
- We don't act like they still "owe" us for what they did wrong.
- And we don't dig up what they did—and remind them about what they did—or slander them by telling others.

That's not how we forgive. When we truly forgive someone, we don't dig up their wrongs again. Like this beef, if we do dig something up that we've supposedly forgiven, it really stinks!

Lessons from a Light Stick

THEME: Read your Bible regularly

THINGS YOU'LL NEED

- ☐ Glow stick for you and each of the kids. Pick up a variety of colors and shapes so no two kids have exactly the same one.
- ☐ Bibles. Gather as many different translations, styles, colors, or special editions as you can, or as many as you have around the house.

Advance Prep

After picking up the glow sticks at the dollar store, there is no advance prep needed.

Running the Activity

- Spread the selection of glow sticks out on the table and invite each of the kids to choose one.

- Hold up a glow stick in its packaging. Explain that a light stick looks good in its wrapper. It's appealing. Designed to attract people to buy it. But if you *leave* a light stick in its packaging, it will never do what it was manufactured to do . . . *shine*.

- Ask each of them to take their glow stick out of the packaging, and do the same.

- Explain how a glow stick works. There is one chemical in the plastic tube, and suspended in that chemical is a glass vial containing a second chemical. You must bend the tube far enough to break that vial inside, allowing the chemical inside it to release. Finally, you shake the light stick to mix the two chemicals thoroughly—and you get this terrific glow.

- Let's all do that now. (Crack the glow sticks to activate them.)

- Unless you get the light stick out of its packaging—and unless you crack it open—you'll never enjoy the glow, right?

Now you're ready to move on. You may want to hit the room lights if it is dark outside and teach the rest of the lesson by the glow of the light sticks. Kids often talk more if it's dark—especially older kids.

Teaching the Lesson

Glow sticks are packaged in many ways, with different shapes, colors, and sizes. Our Bible is like a light stick in some ways. In fact, our Bible comes packaged in hundreds of ways too.

- Different colors and sizes—and unique graphics for each
- Hard cover, paperback, leather bound
- Study editions, red letter editions, student editions
- Dozens of translations and paraphrases
- Illustrated
- Big-print editions
- One-year Bibles

But these differences are primarily about the packaging. These are all about the stuff publishers use to attract you to buy their Bible.

There is so much more to a light stick than its packaging—the really exciting thing is when you crack it and see it glow.

And that is infinitely more true about the Bible. Your Bible won't do what it was created to do—you'll gain no advantage from it—until you "crack it open" and see what's inside. That's when the Bible becomes a lamp to guide us in a dark world.

> Your word is a lamp for my feet,
> a light on my path. (Ps. 119:105)

- Can you imagine a mechanic having a complete shop full of tools—and never going inside the shop and using any of them?
- Can you imagine a climber carrying hundreds of feet of rope—but never uncoiling it and using it to keep anyone from falling?
- Can you imagine a scuba diver who has a full tank of air strapped to their back—but who is forced to stay on the surface instead of diving deeper because they never put the mouthpiece in?
- Can you imagine a lumberjack with a new, powerful chainsaw who tries to cut trees down with it—but never fires the thing up?
- Can you imagine someone getting a brand-new car with a full tank of gas—and being content to leave it in the garage without ever starting it up and driving it?
- Can you imagine a family stocking their kitchen full of food, ingredients, and the latest appliances—yet they always go to a fast-food place to eat and never cook?

Ridiculous examples, right? But this is like so many Christians. We have help, comfort, hope, direction, spiritual nourishment, keys for growth, tools for life, insights for happiness—and so much more available to us in this Bible. But people often don't even bother cracking it open. And as a result, they miss all the protection, help, and advantages they would have found there.

God uses many words and phrases to describe the Bible. Here are some of them.

- Alive (Heb. 4:12)
- Powerful (Rom. 1:16)
- A fire (Jer. 23:29)
- A hammer (Jer. 23:29)
- Sharper than a two-edged sword (Heb. 4:12)
- Flawless (2 Sam. 22:31; Prov. 30:5)
- A light for our path and a lamp for our feet (Ps. 119:105)
- Eternal (Luke 21:33)
- The word of life (Phil. 2:16)
- The word of God (Matt. 15:6)

It's as if God himself wants us to know just how powerful and amazing the Bible is just by the different ways he describes it. Doesn't it make sense that we should get into the Word daily? It not only makes sense . . . but is also an absolutely wise thing to do.

> Your commands are always with me
> and make me wiser than my enemies.
> I have more insight than all my teachers,
> for I meditate on your statutes. (Ps. 119:98–99)

Summing It Up

Here is my list of some of the things the Word has given me. Circle any of the ones that apply to you—and add your own—so the kids really get a feel for how important it is to be in their Bible.

- STRENGTH when I was WEAK.
- DIRECTION when I was LOST.
- CLARITY when I was CONFUSED.
- COURAGE when I was AFRAID.
- WISDOM when I had NO ANSWERS.
- PERSPECTIVE when life was HARD.

- COMFORT when I felt LOSS.
- WARNINGS when I was in ERROR.
- ASSURANCE when I had DOUBTS.
- TRUTH when I was believing LIES.
- JOY when I felt I had nothing to be HAPPY ABOUT.
- DRIVE when I was EXHAUSTED.
- VISION when I was IN A FOG.
- LIGHT when I was in DARKNESS.
- PEACE when I was TROUBLED.
- COMPANY when I was LONELY.

Are you getting the idea just how important it is to crack open your Bible and read it? Can you imagine all the things I would have missed if I didn't read my Bible?

And I don't want you to miss any of these things either.

Here's just a few more "can you imagine" scenarios.

- Can you imagine someone lost in the wilderness—but never opening their survival pack to see what's inside?
- Can you imagine a ship captain crossing the ocean—but never looking at their compass?
- Can you imagine me having a pizza delivered—but never opening the box so we could all enjoy some?

Yeah, more crazy examples. But no less crazy than if you have this Bible but never crack it open and let it light your way through life.

This would be a perfect time to talk to each of the kids about some kind of daily Bible reading plan. If they're too young for that, be sure you're reading some verses to them each day. And remember . . . they learn by example. If they see you cracking open the Word yourself daily, it will go a long way toward influencing them to do the same as they grow up.

Kryptonite and Christians

THEME: Avoid the things that can weaken or destroy us

 THINGS YOU'LL NEED

☐ Superman memorabilia . . . a lunch box, a comic book, even pictures pulled from online. Ask friends. You'd be surprised how many people have something around the house with Superman on it. You can even use YouTube clips from the old black-and-white *Superman* TV series, cartoons, or one of the many movies made.

☐ Kryptonite . . . not actual kryptonite, of course, but anything that will represent it. Paint a rock green. Use a green marble. I used a green laser pointer and shone it through a hunk of crystal. I got both of these fairly cheap online—and it looked fantastic. If you're looking for crystal online, actually search under "kryptonite" and you'll find some great options. If you pick up some kind of kryptonite crystal or whatever, consider getting one for you and each of the kids. You'll use those later as reminders.

☐ Rattrap . . . just like a traditional mousetrap—only bigger. You don't absolutely need this, but it will make the lesson more visual. That's exactly what you want. And you'll also use rattraps for lesson 52, so it doesn't hurt to pick some up. The type you want has a wooden base with a spring-loaded kill bar.

Advance Prep

Get familiar with the rattrap, if you're going to use one. Hold the base in one hand, lift the metal kill bar, and let it snap closed. The key is to hold the trap in a way so you don't catch your fingers. Practice that a bit so you can do it with the kids when you're teaching the lesson.

If you picked up the green laser, put the batteries in and test it on the crystal or whatever you picked up to simulate the kryptonite.

If you're going to actually show the *Superman* TV show or movie clips from an online source, be sure to have that all sorted out in advance so you're not fumbling when you're teaching the lesson. It would be ideal if you used a clip of him around kryptonite.

Running the Activity

Sit the kids down and talk about Superman . . . a fictional hero.

- Show the pictures and memorabilia you have.
- Show the video clips if you plan to do that.
- Talk about how Superman is the ultimate hero. He can do just about anything.
- Ask if anybody knows what Superman's big weakness is.
- Show them your "kryptonite" sample.

You're ready to teach the lesson!

Teaching the Lesson

- Kryptonite could weaken or destroy Superman. If he got near kryptonite, he wouldn't be a hero anymore. He wouldn't be able to help anyone.

- How careful do you think Superman was to stay away from kryptonite?

- What do you think Superman's enemies used when they wanted to destroy him?

- Do you suppose they ever disguised kryptonite—hoping Superman wouldn't realize the danger until he'd already gotten too close?

Yes, Superman's enemies knew his weakness—and they often tried to expose him to the deadly kryptonite.

And we have an enemy too. The devil and his demons. And we don't have just one weakness—like Superman with kryptonite. There are many things that could weaken or destroy us. The enemy knows this, and he has all kinds of traps set for us. Traps that will keep us from living the Christian life we want to live. Traps that will keep us from being a good example to others.

(Pull out the rattrap—and snap the kill bar for a nice effect.)

I have a rattrap here. It's just a visual reminder that our enemy knows our weaknesses. And he will set traps for us. How does the enemy disguise his traps to make them look like something good?

- Sometimes video games can seem harmless and fun—but they can be addicting when we spend too much time playing. That can be like kryptonite.

- Sometimes being on our computer or phone can seem like fun—but we can spend so much time on them that we rarely read the Bible for ourselves. That can be like kryptonite.

- Sometimes we start out looking at things online that are silly or fun—but it can lead to seeing images that inflame us with curiosity for things that are wrong and give us a desire to view more. That can be like kryptonite.

- Drugs or alcohol can look like fun. They can appear harmless. It may seem like we can handle them. But they are kryptonite.

- Sometimes certain friendships can be destructive. Maybe those friends encourage us to do things we know are wrong. Maybe they make us move farther from God rather than closer to him. They are kryptonite.

- When we're of the age to date, or at least are very interested in the opposite sex, we can meet someone who is nice and sweet and considerate and fun—but either they aren't a believer or their faith doesn't have the priority in their life that it should. They can draw us slowly away from the Lord and cool our dedication to him. They can be like kryptonite.

The enemy has all kinds of ways of disguising kryptonite. His goal is to weaken or destroy us.

Do you suppose Superman ever tried to see how close he could get to kryptonite without it destroying him? That would be crazy, right? But instead of staying far away, often Christians deliberately get close to the traps that can hurt them.

The fact is Superman remained a hero because he avoided kryptonite. And if the kryptonite was disguised to look like something harmless, he struggled to get away from it the moment he realized what it truly was.

We can learn a lesson from Superman when it comes to avoiding things we know are bad for us. And generally we know, right? We know when we're moving off God's path for us—and walking toward something that isn't good for us. Listen to this verse. It uses the word *prudence*—which simply means being careful, cautious, and sensible.

> Whoever strays from the path of prudence
>   comes to rest in the company of the dead. (Prov. 21:16)

There's some creepy truth there, right? If you choose to be careless and stray off the path that you know is right, you'll hurt yourself. You're walking right into the enemy's trap.

Summing It Up

Superman is a fictional character known all over the world for being a hero who helps others. If he'd gotten tangled up with kryptonite, his hero days would've been over.

And the same goes for us. The enemy wants to trap us. He's going to offer things that we like. Things we're curious about. He's going to tempt us with a chance to shortcut God's plan. It's a trap. Kryptonite. Don't let him destroy you—or the future you have of helping others.

> Don't let anyone look down on you because you are young, but set an example for the believers in speech, in conduct, in love, in faith and in purity. (1 Tim. 4:12)

If you picked up some kind of "kryptonite" for each of the kids, this is the time to give it to them. Ask them to put it on their desk or bookshelf—or in their backpack or drawer. Let it be a reminder every time they see it to avoid the traps that can weaken or destroy them.

The Seen and Unseen

THEME: We can't see the devil and his demons . . . but they exist

THINGS YOU'LL NEED

☐ Black light . . . you can find them in fluorescent tube or lightbulb varieties to fit in a fixture you already have, or you can find a black light (also spelled blacklight) that comes in a flashlight form. I bought a fluorescent fixture with about an 18-inch black light bulb in it. It worked great because of its portability. I could do this lesson during the day just by plugging the fixture in the bathroom where there are no windows.

☐ Baking flour . . . just a handful is enough

☐ $20 bill, the type with the security stripe imbedded in the paper

☐ Other materials that will glow under the black light. See "Advance Prep" below.

Advance Prep

After picking up your black light, you'll need to experiment before doing this lesson with the kids. The idea is to show your kids that there are things that exist right before our eyes—yet we don't notice them until we look at them in a different light. So your job is to find things that will pop out when viewed with a black light. Things your kids may not notice in daylight or artificial lighting.

Here are some things to try . . .

- **Baking flour.** Put some on the tip of your finger and dab it on a white T-shirt. Try dabbing the flour in the form of a smiley face. The flour will hardly be noticeable until you view the T-shirt under a black light.

- **$20 bill.** You *have* to try this. The little security stripe in the bill normally can't be seen unless you hold the bill up to a light. But under a black light the stripe glows a bright green and is instantly spotted.

- **Honey.** Finger-paint some honey on your arm—or a surface in the room you're in. I wrote the word "hi" on the bathroom counter. When you go dark with the room and bring the black light close, the honey glows.

- **Some cosmetics glow.** Try some on your face and apply the black light test.

- **Clothing.** Use the black light to inspect your blue jeans—especially if they're faded a bit. You'll see strange stains and marks you'd never see with the naked eye. The same goes for shirts and sweaters.

- **White paper, teeth, and so on.** These are things you certainly see in the regular light, but they glow when exposed to a black light.

Experiment. Find some things that work for you. Vaseline (petroleum jelly) works if you apply it just right. Not too thick . . . not too thin. If you're doing this in the bathroom, check out the floor with the black light. Especially around the toilet. Likely you'll see spots or stains that you didn't know existed. Once you've gotten a good mix of things to show the kids, you're ready to go.

Running the Activity

Be sure you've got the kids in a room that can go completely dark. The black light effect will be so much more clear and impressive.

- Show them how *unseen things are seen*—when we use the right light. Things they didn't see in regular light are obviously spotted when viewed solely with the black light (flour on shirt, $20 bill security stripe, honey on the counter, unseen things on clothing, floor, and so on).
- Demonstrate how *different things look* when viewed solely with the black light (teeth, white paper, clothing, and so on).

Teaching the Lesson

Let's talk about some of the things that you didn't see in regular light—things that became extremely obvious under the black light.

- Which of those was your favorite?
- Did anything you saw under the black light surprise you?

Just because we didn't see some of the things in regular light doesn't mean they didn't exist, right? They were there all the time, but only visible under the black light. Would you agree with that?

Let's switch gears here and talk about demons. Some people feel that the devil and his demons don't exist—because they don't see them. But after our fun with the black light, we know there are definitely things that exist—even though we normally can't see them.

How do we know that the devil and his demons are real?

God talks about them in the Bible—and God doesn't lie. And Jesus had many encounters with demons. We read story after story of how he freed people from demons who were making their lives miserable. If demons didn't exist, that would have meant Jesus was deceiving the people.

Often when our world refers to the devil and his demons, they picture them with horns, pitchforks, and red suits. When we use the light of God's Word to see who they really are, we get a very different image.

What do we know about demons?

- They were once angels who joined Satan's rebellion against God (Rev. 12:7–9).

- They can possess unbelievers—and animals—like what is seen in Matthew 8:28–34.

- They cause diseases and disabilities and can mimic mental health issues, disguising their presence. If Jesus said someone had a demon—they had a demon (Mark 5:1–20; Luke 13:11).

- They're disciples of the devil—who is the father of lies, which suggests they're also masters of deception (John 8:44).

- They sometimes cause those they're tormenting to attempt suicide or hurt themselves by cutting or other means (Mark 5:1–5; 9:22).

- They live to distort God's truth, mess up God's people, and keep others from following God (Eph. 6:12; 1 Tim. 4:1).

- They can plant thoughts in your head (Job 4:12–21).

- They possess incredible, supernatural strength (Mark 5:1–4).

- They're terrified of God—and when Jesus gives them a command, they obey (Mark 1:39; James 2:19).

- They're doomed to hell. But until then, they work to deceive people—hoping to drag others to hell with them (Matt. 25:41).

Oh yeah, the devil and his demons are real. The Bible talks plenty about them. How many of them exist? The Bible doesn't say. But it's clear that there are plenty to do the job. And we want to be careful not to underestimate their intelligence. They've existed for thousands of years . . . which means they're likely a whole lot smarter than we are.

So when friends or people you know doubt that demons or the devil exists, remember the little black light experiment. Just because we can't see something with our eyes doesn't mean those things don't exist. And the same holds true for the devil and his demons. When we look with the light of God's Word, we find out pretty quickly that they do exist—and we see them for who they really are.

- Why do you think the devil and his demons want people to believe they don't exist?
- If you walked through a desert canyon loaded with rattlesnakes but truly believed the snakes didn't exist, would you walk through the canyon differently than if you knew rattlers *did* inhabit the area?
- If you didn't believe rattlesnakes existed, you'd let your guard down. And if you let your guard down—you'd be a whole lot more likely to get bit, right?

And that's why the devil and his demons stay under the radar so often. If you don't believe they exist, you'll let your guard down and become an easier target.

Summing It Up

We don't want you to be afraid of demons—because our God is stronger. But we don't want you being misled into thinking they don't exist or that they're harmless either—because that leaves you vulnerable.

Here are three things to remember to avoid getting messed up by demons.

1. **Avoid evil.** Stay away from things you know are wrong. If you play with evil, you're inviting trouble (Prov. 16:17).
2. **Resist.** When you sense the enemy is tempting you, whispering thoughts to discourage or derail or destroy you, or feeding you lies . . . fight back by remembering the truth and running to God (Rom. 12:21; James 4:7–8).
3. **Read the Word.** The enemy is the father of lies. His demons are masters of deception. The Bible is like a light for us as Christians. We must use the light of the Word to help us recognize the work of demons. We must know the truth of God's Word to recognize when the enemy twists that truth (John 8:31–32).

Not Much to Offer

THEME: Give what little you have to God . . . he can make great things from it

THINGS YOU'LL NEED

- [ ] Polymer . . . this is a granular, white powder that is available online at places such as Educational Innovations, Inc. Their website is www .teachersource.com. You can get 100 grams of polymer for about $10, and even this small amount will make about two gallons of "snow."
- [ ] Clear jar . . . something to put the polymer in so the kids can watch it grow. Something like a pickle or jam jar that has been washed clean works fine. If you can soak the label off, that would be great. It will allow a better view of what is going on inside.
- [ ] A ¼ cup measure
- [ ] 16 ounces of water . . . a water bottle works perfectly

Advance Prep

Obviously, you'll need to order the polymer far enough in advance that you'll have time to experiment with it a bit before doing this live with the kids.

- Put ¼ cup of polymer in the jar.
- Add 16 ounces of water and mix quickly.
- Leave the cap off the jar to allow plenty of room for the polymer to grow. This is your opportunity to determine how much polymer you'll want to use with the kids. Ideally, with enough polymer—or a smaller jar—the "snow" you make should fill the jar and spill over the sides.

Fun, right? The kids will love it too.

Running the Activity

Scoop ¼ cup of polymer in the jar, just like you did with your advance prep. Before adding the water, you might ask the kids what they think will happen when you add it.

- Will it make a paste?
- Will the white powder dissolve?

Have one of the kids add and mix in the water. Next, let the kids sit back and watch the polymer expand. Let them run their hands through the powder—noting that there is no sign of the water.

Teaching the Lesson

Once the polymer has stopped growing, you're ready to talk to the kids. You might start out with a question or two.

- Did any of you guess that the white powder would grow?
- Did any of you guess that such a small amount of powder could expand *this* much?

The fact is this polymer grew and expanded a whole lot more than any of us expected. This polymer works so well that it has been used on Hollywood movie sets to create "snow" for films.

The small amount of polymer powder we started with didn't look like much, but when the water was added, it expanded into something far beyond what we might have expected.

This little polymer experiment is a picture of life in some ways. Often, we might see ourselves as being pretty insignificant.

- We don't see ourselves as having any extraordinary talents or abilities.
- We don't see ourselves as having all that much skill in some area—as compared to others.
- We might not see ourselves as being as popular as others—or as having any real friends at all.
- We might not see ourselves as being particularly smart.

Sometimes, at least in some areas of life, we might feel like we don't have much to offer. But just like we didn't predict the effect of the water on the polymer, we can't possibly guess how God can take the little we offer him—and make it grow.

Let's read John 6:1–15 together, and I'm going to ask you some questions afterward.

- How many people needed to be fed?
- Do you think the boy thought his little lunch—packed to feed one person— could possibly feed the crowd?
- Did the *disciples* think what this boy offered could possibly feed the crowd? (Look at verse 9.)
- Did Jesus already have a plan—in advance—with what he would do with the small lunch? (Look at verse 6.)
- Did the boy with the lunch have the ability to expand the lunch himself?
- What is the one thing the boy with the lunch had to do before Jesus set his secret plan into motion?

Yes, the boy had to *offer* the little that he had to Jesus. He gave Jesus everything he possessed—and Jesus did the rest. Nobody else saw the potential in what the boy had to offer, including those close to Jesus. But when that boy gave everything he had to Jesus, a miracle happened that nobody else could have predicted.

You may not feel like much—or that you have much to offer. Have you ever thought of the fact that Jesus already has a plan for how he will use you—and the little you might feel you have to offer—to do important things for him?

What types of things might he be waiting for you to offer him?

- **What about your time?** Especially "free time" that you might use to play games on your phone or whatever.
- **What about your desires?** Have you ever thought of giving your dreams and desires to him—and asking him to plant the desires *he* has for you in your heart?
- **What about your heart?** The boy didn't offer to *split* his lunch. He gave every bit of the lunch he had to Jesus. In our deepest heart, don't you think that's what Jesus wants . . . that we give ourselves completely over to him and his plan?

Think about that boy for a moment. Likely he was hungry, but the word must have gotten out that the Master was looking for food. And this boy was willing to give his lunch to Jesus. What would that boy have missed if he hadn't offered what he had to Jesus?

Summing It Up

When somebody tells you something multiple times, usually that's a sign that what they're saying is important—and they want to be sure you get it. This story of the boy with the loaves and fish is repeated in all four Gospels: Matthew, Mark, Luke, and John. Not every one of the stories of Jesus's life and ministry are found in all of the Gospels like this. This repetition is likely meant for emphasis. God wants to make sure we get the simple lessons of this story. And one clear lesson in it is the importance of giving God all you have.

No matter how little you think you have to offer, trust that God has a plan for how he will use it. Even if you don't see your "potential," and others around you don't seem to either, remember, God has a plan. Give what you've got to Jesus—and trust that he'll do something special with it.

And one more thing. Once the boy gave Jesus his lunch, he never tried to take it back. We need to remember the same thing. If you offer yourself or something you have to Jesus—for him to do with as he sees best—resist the urge to take it back. Leave your life, or whatever you offered him, in his hands.

Fiction Filter

THEME: **The Word is our source of truth in a world of lies**

THINGS YOU'LL NEED

☐ ÖKO H2O Level-2 Advanced Filtration Water Bottle . . . you may already have a similar product—and that may work perfectly. I've seen this particular one in action—which is why I listed its brand and model name. And this is the brand that was used on the International Space Station—so it has a great reputation. Check out some of the demo videos online. You can buy this online for about $30—and you'll probably get some great use out of it, besides the mileage you'll get from it in this devotional! Be sure to get the Level 2 filter model, though. It is more effective than the Level 1.

☐ Coca-Cola . . . a can or personal bottle is all you'll need

☐ Clear drinking glass . . . the fact that it is clear is important. You want to see the difference in the color of the Coke after it's been filtered. You may want a clear glass for each of the kids.

Advance Prep

Once you've got the water bottle in hand, it's time to test it. Remove the ÖKO filter screw-cap and pour several ounces of the Coke into the water bottle. Now screw the cap back in place, turn the water bottle upside down, and squeeze the water bottle. The Coke coming out, after passing through the filter, should be clear. Amazing, right?

You also may want to pick up some specs on your water bottle. Note the types of *unseen* things it filters out. You'll use that information when you do this with the kids.

Running the Activity

Let the kids repeat the steps you did when you tested this out in advance. We want them to be hands-on as much as possible. So opening the Coke, pouring it into the water bottle, and then squeezing it into a clear glass should all be done by the kids. If you have clear glasses for each of the kids, you may want to give each of the kids a turn to squeeze some of the filtered Coke into their glass.

If they'd like to sample how it tastes, that's fine. After they've done that, you're ready to teach them a spiritual truth.

Teaching the Lesson

Clean water is a huge issue in our world. It may not seem like a big deal to us, because we have easy access to clean, pure water. But in some areas of the world, the lack of clean water results in kids and adults getting sick or dying—every day. Without clean, safe water . . . we would all get sick or die.

What this water-purifying bottle did with the Coke was impressive. We could *see* the difference after the Coke passed through the filter.

But a good water-filtering bottle or pitcher does so much more—by removing nasty things that we *don't* see. Bacteria. Parasites. There are harmful contaminants in water—even out of the tap—that are invisible to the eye. A water bottle like this is designed to filter out those nasty elements and leave you with safe drinking water. This bottle can be a great survival tool. In fact, if every person in the world had—and used—a bottle like this, there would be a lot less sickness and death.

There is a parallel to the spiritual life that I want to share with you. Water is something that we take into our bodies in some way every day of our lives. If that water is not pure, our health will be impacted in a negative way.

Similarly, there is information we "ingest" in our minds every day—just like our bodies take in water. Information comes from many sources. News, media, school, friends, and more. But how do we know if the information we absorb is good and pure?

- In other words, how do we know if the information we receive is true?
- And how do we separate what is true from what is not?

If we drink in this bad information—and think it is true—it will impact every aspect of our lives.

- How we *think*.
- How we *act*.
- How we *speak*.
- How we *treat others*.
- How we form our *attitudes*, *opinions*, and our *perspective* in life.

Like unfiltered water contains invisible contaminants, often what the world tells us is contaminated with subtle lies. Things we as Christians think are bad and wrong, the world will often tell us are really good and right. And things Christians believe are good and right, the world will often tell us are bad and wrong. Some of these lies from the world are so convincing that Christians swallow them without even thinking about it.

How do we know what is truth and what is fiction in the information we're bombarded with every day? God gave us the Bible to do exactly that. Think of the Word as a highly effective *filtration* system. When we read the Word, it helps us separate the truth from the lies. We can trust that what God says in his Word is the truth. In fact, when Jesus was being questioned by Pilate just before the crucifixion, he explained that one of the reasons he came to earth was to bring us truth.

> Jesus answered, "You say that I am a king. In fact, the reason I was born and came into the world is to testify to the truth. Everyone on the side of truth listens to me." (John 18:37)

Earlier, Jesus told his followers to grab on to what he taught—because he taught truth.

> To the Jews who had believed him, Jesus said, "If you hold to my teaching, you are really my disciples. Then you will know the truth, and the truth will set you free." (8:31–32)

And shortly before Jesus was crucified, he prayed for his followers. And there he made it clear that the Bible is our source of truth.

> My prayer is not that you take them out of the world but that you protect them from the evil one. They are not of the world, even as I am not of it. Sanctify them by the truth; your word is truth. (17:15–17)

The Bible refers to the devil as the "father of lies." And the devil and his demons are really good at getting people to believe his lies. We need to be in the Word so that we immediately recognize truth—and don't get fooled by the devil's lies. Being in the Word helps us distinguish fact from fiction.

Summing It Up

How crazy would it be to have a filtration water bottle like this—and never use it, even though we know the water we're drinking is contaminated? That would be insane, right?

And it is the same with us. We know the world is feeding us lies—even if we don't see them—about life and how to live it. If we deliberately ignore the Word, if we don't use the Bible as our filter to keep out the wrong attitudes, opinions, and so forth, we're opening ourselves up to nasty contaminants and spiritual sickness in many ways.

Psalm 119 asks the question of how to keep oneself pure in a contaminated world. The answer? Live according to how the Bible tells us to live.

> How can a young person stay on the path of purity?
> By living according to your word. (v. 9)

Staying in God's Word helps us filter out the lies from what is true—and that will definitely make the quality of our spiritual lives better. King David prayed that God would guide him as he did that—and that's a pretty good idea for us to do too . . . don't you think?

> Guide me in your truth and teach me,
> for you are God my Savior,
> and my hope is in you all day long. (Ps. 25:5)

Pressure Cooker

THEME: Do we have an anger problem? Pressure situations are the true test

THINGS YOU'LL NEED

☐ Ivory bar soap, at least two bars—one to practice with in advance and one to use with the kids. *Better yet*, have one bar for each of the kids. And you'll want to stick with the Ivory brand for this. The unique way Ivory is manufactured is what makes this work.

☐ Plates . . . paper or ceramic is fine, as long as they are microwave-safe

☐ Access to a microwave oven

Advance Prep

Take one of the bars of Ivory soap, peel off the wrapper, and place it on a plate. Now set the microwave to cook for five minutes. You won't need all that time, but at least the microwave won't stop until you're finished.

At first nothing happens, but the heat of the microwave soon makes the bar of soap go berserk in entertaining ways. Foamy shoots or roots will seemingly burst out of the soap in random ways.

When the expanding soap seems to slow or stop—or when you think you've seen enough—turn off the microwave. You're ready for the kids.

Running the Activity

Give each of the kids a bar of Ivory soap and a plate. Ask them to unwrap the bar of soap and set it in the center of the plate.

Now, one at a time, microwave each bar of soap until it expands in all kinds of freaky, weird ways.

When you're done, you may even ask the kids to judge which bar of soap looks the funniest. Now you're ready to move on.

Teaching the Lesson

Watching this soap explode in these strange ways was fun. But there's another kind of explosion that isn't so fun to watch . . . and it happens with people all the time. I'm talking about when people explode in anger.

When we put the soap in the microwave, strange growths burst out in all directions. What kinds of strange things do seemingly absolutely normal people do when they get angry?

- Do perfectly sane people start yelling or saying mean, nasty things?
- Do others go silent and hardly speak?
- Do some get all red in the face?
- Do some stomp out of the room and slam the door?
- Do some refuse to look at you when they're angry?
- Do others get in your face?
- Do some cry when they're angry?
- Do others make people around them cry?
- Do some slam their fist into something—like a wall?

- Do others slam their fist into *people*?
- Do some throw things?

There are all kinds of things people do when they're angry. And usually these things make them look as weird as a bar of Ivory soap that's been in the microwave too long. Often, an angry person says and does things that they regret later—or should. Anger often expresses itself in some really out-of-control ways.

- When a person loses their temper, how does that show they have a lack of self-control?
- What role do you think pride has when it comes to someone losing their temper?
- What type of "pressure cooker" situations tend to make it easier to lose your temper? When you're tired? Hungry? Overwhelmed with homework?
- Are there ways you can avoid being in a pressure cooker or microwave situation?

Sometimes anger is okay—as long as it doesn't lead us into doing something wrong. But that type of anger is pretty rare. Usually our anger leads us to do or say something that does not please God. That's the anger we want to look at for a couple of minutes here.

The Bible has a lot to say about that kind of anger.

1. Anger generally makes messes . . . and it doesn't result in us being the kind of Christian God wants us to be.

   My dear brothers and sisters, take note of this: Everyone should be quick to listen, slow to speak and slow to become angry, because human anger does not produce the righteousness that God desires. (James 1:19–20)

2. God would like us to get rid of our unhealthy anger.

   Do not let any unwholesome talk come out of your mouths, but only what is helpful for building others up according to their needs, that it may benefit those who listen. And do not grieve the Holy Spirit of God, with whom you were sealed for the day of redemption. Get rid of all bitterness, rage and anger, brawling and slander, along with every form of malice. Be kind and compassionate to one another, forgiving each other, just as in Christ God forgave you. (Eph. 4:29–32)

3. Being angry is not wise.

Fools give full vent to their rage,
　　but the wise bring calm in the end. (Prov. 29:11)

4. God can help us control unhealthy anger.

But the fruit of the Spirit is love, joy, peace, forbearance, kindness, goodness, faithfulness, gentleness and self-control. Against such things there is no law. (Gal. 5:22–23)

Summing It Up

We may *seem* to have anger under control. But what about when the "heat is on" in some area of our lives? That's the true test of whether we have problems with anger or not.

If we *do* have some anger issues, or have outbursts of embarrassing anger, we lack self-control. And self-control is one of the things the Holy Spirit gives us as we surrender more to him . . . and as we ask him for it.

And pride, being another root that feeds anger, is a heart issue. Ask the Holy Spirit to change your heart—and you'll find that he does that too.

People who get angry do some pretty weird things. And often they hurt themselves and others as a result. It can be hard to stop and ask God to help keep you from getting angry when you already *are* angry. The best time to ask for his help is *before* you are angry . . . like right now. Would you ask God to change your heart—and give you self-control so that you don't get so angry?

And if you ask God to do that, remember to keep asking him for help. When you feel yourself getting angry, some people recommend you stop and count to ten. That doesn't do much good, honestly. But when you feel yourself getting angry, take a moment to talk to God. Ask him to change your heart. To remove your pride. To change your perspective and to give you self-control so you don't do something that would disappoint him. Do you think that is the kind of prayer he will honor? I'm sure of it.

Barfing Bucket

THEME: Being dishonest and compromising instead of doing what we know to be right

 THINGS YOU'LL NEED

This is quite a list of supplies. And some of the items are a little pricey, so if you can go in with some other families to pick this stuff up, great. While this object lesson requires more supplies than most in this book, it's also a powerful lesson . . . so if you can swing this one, do it.

One other thought. If you know a teacher, often they can loan you a number of the things you'll need, such as beakers, graduated cylinders, and a gram scale. Or give them the potassium iodide and let them weigh out the proper amount on a gram scale and give it back to you in a plastic bag. Some libraries even have science lab items like these for homeschool groups to check out.

- ☐ Five-gallon plastic bucket and lid, available at any hardware store
- ☐ Utility knife or box cutter

☐ 27 percent hydrogen peroxide solution, sold in pool supplies stores as "pool shock." Now, there are different types of pool shock, but for this lesson, you must get this strong hydrogen peroxide solution. Be sure to check the label. I get mine at Leslie's Pool Supplies, www .lesliespool.com. Here is the product name as they stock it: "Chlorine-Free BAQUACIL swimming pool OXIDIZER STEP 2." They've got stores nationwide, and you can order online.

KEEP IT SAFE

This hydrogen peroxide is much stronger than what you buy in the drug store—so you'll need to wear chemical-resistant rubber gloves and safety glasses.

☐ Potassium iodide . . . get this online as well. You won't need much. You'll use only about 10 grams per demo. That's about a teaspoonful. And there are different "grades" of this chemical. You don't need the "lab grade." A lesser grade works just fine. And you can get it either in a granular form or in a chunk form that you can grind up later.

☐ Liquid dish soap . . . you won't need much of this

☐ Chemical-resistant rubber gloves . . . these are a must for each of the kids helping

☐ Safety glasses . . . these are another must for each of the kids—and yourself. You don't want any of this stuff splashing in your eyes—especially when you're cleaning up.

☐ Two clean, clear jars or beakers. One that would hold about 400 milliliters is great, if you get beakers. If you use jars, a medium-size pickle jar is about right.

☐ Graduated cylinder. You'll need to measure out 200 milliliters of the pool shock, so order yourself a plastic graduate that has measurements up to 400 or 500 milliliters.

- [ ] Smaller graduated cylinder. You'll need to measure 15 milliliters of water and 10 milliliters of liquid dish soap. So you'll need this second, smaller graduate with finer markings on it to get the measurements right.

- [ ] Gram scale. You can get these cheap at places like American Science and Surplus, www.sciplus.com. If you can't get a gram scale, you can substitute it with a 1 teaspoon measuring spoon. (One level teaspoon of potassium iodide is close to ten grams.)

- [ ] Plastic catch basin . . . you're going to create a lot of foam with this little experiment, so you'll need something to catch it in so it doesn't go all over the floor.

- [ ] Plastic sheeting . . . if you do this indoors, you'll want to put some plastic sheeting on the table and floor. This solution stains almost immediately when it touches something. You can pick up the plastic in the paint section of the hardware store.

Advance Prep

After you get your supplies, you'll need to do one more thing before you test this: cut a face in the five-gallon bucket you picked up. Find a friend who has a heat gun. If you know someone who does flooring, they've probably got one. Draw a face on the bucket with a marker, then heat the spots and use the utility knife to cut out the face. Once the bucket is heated, it will cut like butter.

When cutting the face, think of a jack-o'-lantern. Get a nice big smile on this thing—and make it close to the bottom of the bucket. Cut an easy triangle nose, and you can do the same with the eyes. The key is to keep that mouth low on the bucket, and the top of the eyes shouldn't be more than two-thirds of the way up the bucket. You don't want the eyes anywhere near the top of the bucket.

Next, be sure to try the experiment on your own, without the kids, prior to your devotions time with them. And when you do this, be sure to wear safety glasses and chemical-resistant rubber gloves. The first time I did this, I did it outside near the hose for easy clean up. If you do this indoors for your debut run, be sure the plastic and the catch basin are in place. I've seen this solution stain tile floors—so be careful.

Here are the two ingredients for the first beaker or glass jar. Mix these both in the same container.

- 200 milliliters of the hydrogen peroxide solution (pool shock)
- 10 milliliters of liquid dish soap

Here are the two ingredients for the second beaker or glass jar. Mix these two ingredients into the second beaker or glass jar until all the potassium iodide crystals or chunks are completely dissolved.

- 10 grams of the potassium iodide, weighed out on your gram scale
- 15 milliliters of water

Now, set the five-gallon bucket on the edge of a table, with the face you cut into it facing out so that any foam gushing out of the eyes, nose, and mouth will drop in the catch basin you've positioned on the floor below.

Set the first beaker with the hydrogen peroxide / dish soap mix inside the bucket. When you're ready, pour the potassium iodide and water solution into the beaker of hydrogen peroxide.

You should see a dark foam rising up out of the beaker. Now, place the lid on the bucket. You don't have to snap it in place, just set it on top to keep the foam from overflowing.

The foam will continue to form until it gushes out the open mouth, nose, and eyes of your bucket. You may have to adjust the position of the bucket slightly to make sure the foam is captured by the catch basin below.

Congratulations—you did it! Your kids are going to love this!

Running the Activity

Have all the elements measured out and ready to go in the two beakers or jars before the kids enter the room. You'll want to get right to the lesson—and you'll reduce the chances of an accident or of making a mistake with measurements if everything is all set in advance.

You might start out by pointing at the bucket and saying something like this:

Kids, I'd like you to imagine that this bucket is you. And I have this beaker here with a solution in it (hydrogen peroxide and liquid dish soap). Let's say this represents your heart. And I'm going to say that deep down in your heart you want to be a good person.

- You want to tell the truth.
- You want to do the right things.

So let's put that beaker deep inside you.

Now, as much as you want to tell the truth—as much as you want to do the right things—there is another part of you that doesn't. That is the part of you that is willing to *compromise* at times.

- Sometimes there are things we want to do that we know aren't right.
- Sometimes we lie because we're afraid that we'll really get in trouble if we tell the truth.

But if we do that—if we compromise in our desire to tell the truth and to do the right things—something will almost always happen. Let me demonstrate what I mean.

Let's say this second jar represents "compromise." Now, you can see I have only a little bit of compromise here. But that is all it takes. What if you allow this little bit of compromise into your heart, which really wants to do the right things?

(Pour the potassium iodide solution into the hydrogen peroxide solution and place the lid on the bucket. Now let them watch the foam pouring out. After the foam subsides, then finish the thought with them.)

Here is the truth about compromise. If you allow a little bit of compromise in your convictions . . . likely a whole lot more will follow.

Summing It Up

In the Old Testament, we read about many kings. Most of them messed up really bad. They compromised when it came to doing what was right—and generally their compromise wasn't limited to one isolated incident. Once they compromised, it seemed that a whole lot more compromise followed. King after king made the mistake of compromising—and paying a high price for it.

One such king was Rehoboam, the son of King Solomon of Israel. He did evil, wrong things—and paid a heavy price for his compromising. In this passage, God reveals a secret as to why this king compromised.

> King Rehoboam established himself firmly in Jerusalem and continued as king. He was forty-one years old when he became king, and he reigned seventeen years in Jerusalem, the city the LORD had chosen out of all the tribes of Israel in which to put his Name. His mother's name was Naamah; she was an Ammonite. He did evil because he had not set his heart on seeking the LORD. (2 Chron. 12:13–14)

Did you catch that last line? He did evil because he didn't set his heart on seeking God. When is the time to make a decision about whether you'll follow God's ways—or compromise? Long before you're tempted, right? Apparently, King Rehoboam didn't do that. He decided to do what he felt like at the time. That is a formula for compromise—and disaster.

Do you want to be one who follows God and his ways? Make a decision to do the right things. To tell the truth. And ask God to help you stick to that conviction.

There is a great little prayer in Psalm 119 that expresses that desire to set your heart on seeking God and obeying his Word. Listen to what this Scripture says . . . and I hope you'll make it your prayer too.

> My heart is set on keeping your decrees
> to the very end. (v. 112)

Set your heart on seeking God and not compromising. Make it a foundational conviction of your life. And make this conviction not just for today or this week but, as it says here in this psalm, "to the very end."

Watch Your Step

THEME: The role of parents is to guide and protect their kids. Parents aren't trying to cramp your style . . . they're trying to keep you from becoming crippled

 ## THINGS YOU'LL NEED

- ☐ Rattraps, available at any hardware store. You're looking for the traditional type. Wood base. Nasty spring-loaded kill bar. They look just like mousetraps, only bigger. I picked up a pack of Victor brand traps, and they work great. One trap is enough to teach the lesson, but having more traps might help you make your point better. If you buy enough traps to give each of the kids one after the lesson, they'll have a nice reminder of what you taught them.
- ☐ Blindfold, or a scarf works fine
- ☐ Wood pencils . . . only if you want to demonstrate the traps

Advance Prep

After you've purchased the rattrap, get familiar with it a bit. Later, when you're with the kids, you'll want to demonstrate the power of the rattrap. There are a couple of potential ways to do that.

1. Hold the trap in one hand, pull back the spring-loaded kill bar a couple inches, and, *making sure no fingers are in the way*, let it snap closed. It makes a nice, loud bang. This is an effective way to demonstrate the power of the rattrap to the kids.

2. The other way is to actually set—*and trip*—the trap. Set the trap on the floor. Carefully pull back the kill bar all the way. Then hold the kill bar in place with the tripping mechanism. Once the trap is set, take a pencil and deliberately press the bait pad to trip the release mechanism. The key is to hold the pencil firmly in place against the bait pad. As long as you don't let the pencil get brushed out of the way, the kill bar should slam into the pencil with enough force to snap it in two.

After you've chosen and practiced which method you'd like to use, you're ready to do this with the kids.

Running the Activity

You'll want to start out by showing the kids the rattrap—and demonstrating its power in whichever way you feel most comfortable. If you're going to snap the pencil, I'd suggest you have the trap all set before they get in the room rather than trying to do it with the kids pressing in to see.

Whether you snap the trap or snap the pencil, they'll get a feel for how much that trap would hurt if they stepped in it.

If you have multiple traps, you can set the traps up in a maze across the floor. If not, just talk them through it.

- Imagine I had each of you take off your shoes and socks and had a whole maze of rattraps set up across the floor.

- What if I asked for one of you to volunteer . . . and I blindfolded you (actually blindfold one of the kids), spun you around a few times, and had you march—not shuffle—right through that maze of traps?
- Very soon you would hear this (snap a trap in your hand like you practiced), and you'd be in a world of pain, right?

Now, if I really *did* ask for one of you to volunteer to go barefoot and blindfolded into that maze of traps—you wouldn't do it, would you? Nobody wants their toes in one of these traps.

- But what if we did it a little differently?
- What if you were still barefoot and blindfolded, but I had you face me and put your hands on my shoulders—and I put mine on yours.
- What if I carefully led you through the maze? Would you be more likely to go through it then?

You might be a little scared, but if you really trusted me, you could be sure I would get you through that maze without you getting caught in any traps.

This whole rattrap activity is a picture of life. There are traps out there in our world. Nasty ones that can hurt you. Can you think of any?

- Drugs
- Alcohol
- Friends who aren't a good influence
- Smartphones used unwisely
- Too much time playing computer games
- Skipping time reading your Bible
- Wrong attitudes
- Pornography
- Choosing to live a secret life—hiding sin instead of dealing with it

The devil and his demons have all kinds of traps out there—just hoping you'll step in one. And if you do, you'll be in a lot of pain. The pain may be delayed—like the pain of regret. But pain always follows after sin.

But God doesn't want you to step in traps. He doesn't want you to hurt yourself—and others—like you will if you step in a trap.

That's one reason he gives you a mom. That's one reason he gives you a dad.

- A parent's job is to *provide* for their kids.
- A parent's job is to *prepare* their kids for the future—especially spiritually.
- A parent's job is to *protect* their kids—both now and for the future.

As you get older, the danger and intensity of the traps increase too. But God doesn't want you to go through these years all by yourself. That is one reason he has me here. I'm to guide you through the maze of traps.

So sometimes I'm going to say no to things you really want to do. I'm not trying to be mean. I'm trying to protect you from traps that you might not see. I'm trying to do the job God gave me to do . . . and with God's help, I want to do it the best I possibly can.

If you think I'm being unfair, talk to me. And try to understand that sometimes I may still have to say no so that I *provide, prepare,* and *protect* you the way I believe God wants me to.

Here are some Scripture verses that help express my heart on this.

> In the paths of the wicked are snares and pitfalls,
>> but those who would preserve their life stay far from them. (Prov. 22:5)

I love you like crazy, and my desire is that I help keep you away from the paths where there are traps. Your life could depend on this.

> Hold on to instruction, do not let it go;
>> guard it well, for it is your life.
> Do not set foot on the path of the wicked
>> or walk in the way of evildoers.
> Avoid it, do not travel on it;
>> turn from it and go on your way. (4:13–15)

As a parent, this is my prayer. That you'll take what I've taught you—and that I'll continue to teach—and hold on to it. Guard it. Live by it. And avoid the paths that lead to doing wrong things. Those paths are loaded with traps.

Don't let anyone look down on you because you are young, but set an example for the believers in speech, in conduct, in love, in faith and in purity. (1 Tim. 4:12)

First Timothy 4:12 is another prayer I have for you. Not just that you'll avoid the traps—and let me help you do that—but that you'll be an example of what a follower of Christ should be in the way you love others, in the way you talk, in the things you choose to do, in the way you choose to live a pure life, and in the way you trust God.

Summing It Up

Sometimes you hear these verses from the Bible quoted . . . reminding you about how you're to obey your parents.

Children, obey your parents in the Lord, for this is right. "Honor your father and mother"—which is the first commandment with a promise—"so that it may go well with you and that you may enjoy long life on the earth." (Eph. 6:1)

I never want to use a verse like this in a negative way. It is a positive thing. Sure, it can be really hard to obey parents at times—especially when we say no to something you really want to do.

But this verse is a reminder to hang in there. To trust God with this—and to trust your parents. And if you honor and obey your parents, I can guarantee you're going to avoid some really nasty traps out there. That alone will be one way that things will "go well with you," as the verse promises. You'll avoid the pain and regret of stepping into traps.

Will you do that? Trust God . . . trust me . . . and we'll both help you avoid some traps—and make your life a lot better in the process.

Tim Shoemaker is the author of fourteen books and is a popular speaker at conferences and schools around the country. Over twenty-five years of working with kids and youth has helped him relate to his reading and listening audience in a unique way. He is a regular contributor to *Focus On the Family Clubhouse* and *Clubhouse JR* magazines. His contemporary suspense novel, *Code of Silence*, was named in the "Top Ten Crime Novels for Youth" by Booklist.

Tim has learned firsthand the need to do more than talking at kids—if you want to hold their attention. And he has found how powerfully object lessons and activities work to convey truth in ways kids never forget. Happily married for over thirty-eight years, Tim has three grown sons and three daughters-in-law, lives in Rolling Meadows, Illinois—and still loves working with youth.

CONNECT WITH **TIM SHOEMAKER** AT
TimShoemakerSmashedTomatoes.com

 @TimShoemaker1    @AuthorTimShoemaker    @TimShoemaker1